ARMED & DANGEROUS

The 2011 Phillies:
Perfectly Pitched
& Poised to Dominate

FRAN ZIMNIUCH

TRIUMPH
BOOKS

Philadelphia Phillies starting pitchers (from left) Roy Halladay, Joe Blanton, Cliff Lee, Roy Oswalt, and Cole Hamels take part in a joint news conference following their first spring training baseball workout on February 14, 2011.

Copyright © 2011 by Triumph Books

No part of this publication may be reproduced, stored in a retrieval system, or transmitted in any form by any means, electronic, mechanical, photocopying, or otherwise, without the prior written permission of the publisher, Triumph Books, 542 South Dearborn Street, Suite 750, Chicago, Illinois 60605. Triumph Books and colophon are registered trademarks of Random House, Inc.

This book is available in quantity at special discounts for your group or organization. For further information, contact:

Triumph Books
542 South Dearborn Street
Suite 750
Chicago, Illinois 60605
(312) 939–3330
Fax (312) 663–3557

www.triumphbooks.com

Printed in U.S.A.
ISBN: 978-1-60078-643-3

Content packaged by Mojo Media, Inc.
Joe Funk: Editor
Jason Hinman: Creative Director

Interior photos courtesy of AP Images

Front cover main image and Cole Hamels inset photo courtesy of Getty Images
Cliff Lee and Roy Oswalt inset photos courtesy of AP Images
Back cover photo courtesy of US Presswire

contents

Chapter 1: A Whimper and a Bang!..................7
Chapter 2: R2C2—Arms Control 19
Chapter 3: The Bullpen..................61
Chapter 4: The Starting Eight—Plus..................81
Chapter 5: Charlie Manuel—The Skipper..................117
Phils Trivia Tester..................127

Armed & Dangerous

1

A Whimper and a Bang!

The Phillies' two-year run as National League champions ended with a whimper and a bang. Actually, it was more like a bang followed by a whimper. The bang was a dramatic home run by San Francisco third baseman Juan Uribe against Ryan Madson that broke a 2–2 tie in the eighth inning of Game 6 of the National League Championship Series and landed just above the right-field fence at Citizens Bank Park in Philadelphia. The whimper was the final out of the game an inning later, as Ryan Howard watched a called third strike from San Francisco's bearded closer, Brian Wilson.

Wth that, hopes for a third consecutive visit to the Fall Classic ended and San Francisco celebrated their astounding ascension to National League champs, advancing to the World Series against the Texas Rangers. The Phillies' offense failed them in this contest, going 0-for-9 with runners in scoring position. As a result, the Giants won the game and the National League Championship Series, four games to two. Then they went on to defeat the Rangers in the World Series.

But in spite of the disappointing finale, the season still has to be considered a resounding success story for Philadelphia. The Phillies blazed to a 97–65 record to win the National League East Division crown as 3,777,322 fans crossed through the turnstiles at Citizens Bank Park. For the first time in franchise history, the Phillies had the best record in Major League Baseball.

Newly acquired ace right-hander Roy Halladay led the team with a 21–10 record and a 2.44 ERA with nine complete games. One of those victories occurred on May 29 when the Phillies visited the Florida Marlins. What seemed like a regular game featuring a pitching duel between Halladay and Marlins starter Josh Johnson became less regular with every inning. The only run of the game came in

Ryan Howard reacts after looking at a called third strike in the bottom of the ninth inning of Game 6 of the 2010 National League Championship Series. Giants catcher Buster Posey and closer Brian Wilson celebrate the Giants' first pennant since 2003.

Armed & Dangerous

the visitors' half of the third when Chase Utley hit a drive to center field that clanked off the glove of Cameron Maybin, allowing Wilson Valdez to score from first base.

While Johnson pitched extremely well, Halladay was perfect—literally. He earned his seventh victory of the season as he surrendered no hits, no walks, and no base runners en route to a perfect game. 27 Marlins up, 27 Marlins down. When former Phillie Ronnie Paulino hit a 3–2 breaking ball to Philadelphia third baseman Juan Castro, who wheeled and nailed Paulino at first base, Halladay became the 10th Phillies hurler to throw a no-hitter. He joined Jim Bunning as the only Phillies to have thrown a perfect game. In addition, he would later become the first hurler to throw two no-hitters in the same season since Nolan Ryan did the trick in 1973.

During the course of the regular season, the Phillies played well at times, but were largely inconsistent. As the season wore on they were unable to put a lock on the division. While the team's pitching was strong, the hitting was erratic. At various times during the season Jimmy Rollins (88 games played), Chase Utley (115 games), and Placido Polanco (132 games) missed time in the lineup. To make a strong pitching staff even better and aid the team in its run for the division title, the Phillies dealt promising left-hander J.A. Happ to the Houston Astros' in a deal that would bring the Astros' ace right-hander Roy Oswalt to Philadelphia.

All Oswalt did was jump right into an already impressive rotation and go 7–1 with a 1.74 ERA down the stretch. He helped the team as they climbed the standings. Then, on September 7, with an 8–7 win over Florida coupled with a loss by the upstart Braves, the Phillies retook the division lead for the first time since May 30. A strong September included an 11-game winning streak. The Phillies made some history on September 27 when Halladay pitched them to an 8–0 win over the Washington Nationals, clinching their fourth consecutive National League East title. It marked just the third time in National League history that a team made four consecutive postseason appearances. Charlie Manuel's squad joins the 1991–2005 Atlanta Braves and the 1921–1924 New York Giants.

There were many times during the course of the regular season that history seemed on the side of the Phillies. No wonder that history was also present in the National League Division Series against the Cincinnati Reds. As if his 21 regular season victories and perfect game during the regular season were not enough, Roy Halladay made some more history in Game 1 of the NLDS by throwing a no-hitter against the Reds. The masterpiece gave the Phillies a 1–0 advantage in the best-of-five series and Halladay another place in baseball history, joining Don Larsen as the only pitcher to throw a no-hitter in the postseason.

In Game 2, the offense took advantage of two Cincinnati errors to score five unearned run en route to a 7–4 victory. Lefty Cole Hamels showed his 2008 form with an overpowering five-hit, 2–0 shutout in

Roy Halladay celebrates with catcher Carlos Ruiz after no-hitting the Cincinnati Reds in Game 1 of the 2010 National League Division Series. It marked only the second no-hitter in postseason history.

Armed & Dangerous

The 2011 Phillies: Perfectly Pitched & Poised to Dominate

the third and deciding game of the series to propel the team to the National League Championship Series against the Giants.

Game 1 in Philadelphia saw two of the best pitchers in baseball, Halladay and Tim Lincecum, squared off. The Giants muscled their way to a 4–3 win thanks to a pair of home runs by Cody Ross. Carlos Ruiz and Jayson Werth homered for the Phillies in a losing cause.

Oswalt evened the series at one game apiece allowing just one run over eight strong innings. On the base path, he ran through a stop sign at third base to score one of the runs of the 6–1 Philadelphia win. Ross accounted for the lone San Francisco run with his third homer of the series.

As the series moved to the City by the Bay for Game 3, Matt Cain was brilliant, throwing a three-hit shutout as the Giants took the series lead with a 3–0 win against Hamels. Ross continued his clutch play

(left) Roy Oswalt throws during the first inning of Game 2 of the National League Championship Series. (above) Oswalt slides safely past Giants catcher Buster Posey in the seventh inning of Game 2 of the National League Championship Series, scoring from second on a hit by Placido Polanco.

Armed & Dangerous

driving in one of the runs.

San Francisco took a commanding three-games-to-one lead in the series with a 6–5 win in Game 4. The contest swung back and forth and was knotted up at 5–5 going into the home half of the ninth inning. With Oswalt pitching in relief, Juan Uribe won the game with a walk-off sacrifice fly to give San Francisco a stranglehold on the series.

Philadelphia bounced back with a hard-fought 4–2 win to make it a three-games-to-two series, which would head back to Citizen's Bank Park for Game 6. Staring elimination in the face, Halladay pitched six gutty innings, hampered by a pulled groin muscle. Brad Lidge earned the save and Werth hit another home run. The win set up the final game in Philadelphia which resulted in Uribe's series-winning home run against Madson.

Jamie Moyer has pitched 24 seasons in the major leagues, the better part of the last five with the Phillies. Sidelined with an arm injury, he had been a key contributor to the team over that tenure, sporting a 56–40 record. He was 9–9 in 2010 and will rehab for the 2011 season with a comeback planned for 2012. Not only was the veteran southpaw a valued member of the team on the playing field, but his veteran presence among the rest of the team was a beneficial bonus. His acquisition by the team in 2006 was a pleasant surprise that proved to this native of Souderton, Pennsylvania, that in spite of the prevailing opposing thought, you can go home again.

"It was a dream come true," Moyer said of being able to pitch near his hometown. "Never did I think I'd have the opportunity to pitch in Philadelphia the way my career path was going. I had 10 pretty good years in Seattle but when they were looking to move guys, I was moved to Philadelphia. I really enjoyed my four-plus years with the Phillies. When I first came over, we were trying to catch teams. But that was exciting because I was coming from a last-place team right into a pennant race. And obviously 2007, 2008, 2009, and 2010 speak for themselves as playoff years. To come back to Philly was special and to win a World Series in 2008, well I don't think I could have scripted it any better. Being at the Phillies' parade in 1980 was exciting, but then 28 years later being in the parade was quite special too.

"I would assess the 2010 season as a successful season, but not a completely successful season because we didn't get to and win the World Series," he continued. "With the perfectionists who are in that clubhouse, anything less than a World Series and we didn't achieve our goal. I'm sure that Charlie [Manuel] and the everyday players feel the same way. To get to a World Series and to win a World Series is not that easy. You play those 162 games during the season and a lot of crazy things can happen. That's why they call it baseball."

As the disappointment over the loss settled on the Phillies and their fans, the team remained confident in its ability to bounce back. Sporting a team that included the likes of Howard, Chase Utley, Jimmy Rollins, Shane Victorino, and others, the future still

Jayson Werth, who signed as a free agent with the Washington Nationals after the 2010 season, swings for the fences in Game 5 of the 2010 National League Championship Series.

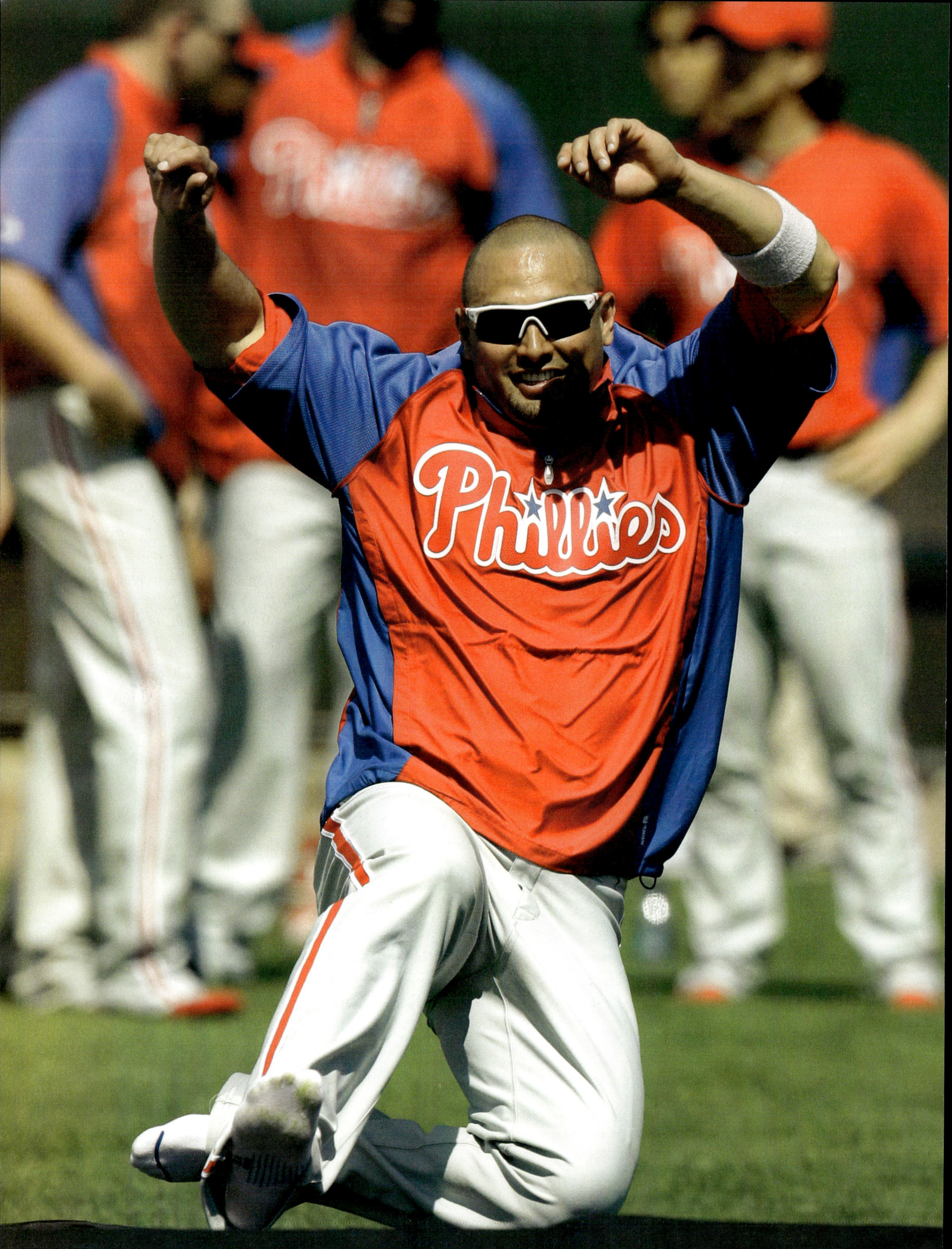
Phillies

The 2011 Phillies: Perfectly Pitched & Poised to Dominate

seemed bright. But at the same time, the certain loss of slugging right fielder Jayson Werth and some questions about the pitching staff beyond Roy Halladay, Cole Hamels, and Roy Oswalt ensured that the winter leading up to the 2011 season would be an interesting one. But very few people could have imagined just how interesting.

"I'd say that disappointment was the No. 1 term to use," said Phillies veteran broadcaster Chris Wheeler, who has spent more than four decades with the organization. "But you have to understand that the players are different from the fans. Fans take it differently. They were really down. But the players just felt that it wasn't the end of the world. Their attitude was that they gave it their best shot, but the Giants beat them. They were thinking that they're still a good team who would get them next year.

"It wasn't like the teams back in 1976, 1977, and 1978, who just couldn't get over the hump and were completely frustrated. It was really different this time and they were confident that they would get them next year. It was totally different from those teams in the '70s. This team had won it all before, they were still together and they were confident that they could do it again."

It was also to be a winter of changes, some with a bang and some a whimper. As expected, the team lost Werth, but quite surprisingly to the Washington Nationals. He parlayed his solid years of service in Philadelphia into a seven-year, $126 million deal with the Nationals. With a bulging budget, the Phillies decided against trying to match the lucrative deal he got from their division rivals from the south. Impressive sub Ben Francisco and young phenom Domonic Brown are both available and may be platooned in right field. Should either one falter, John Mayberry Jr. is also considered a viable alternative. But the quiet loss of Werth was about to be replaced by the latest Big Bang in the City of Brotherly Love.

The starting rotation was solid at the top, anchored by Halladay, Hamels, and Oswalt. Veteran Joe Blanton and young Kyle Kendrick gave the team depth that many teams would love to have. But the party line throughout the early part of the off-season, that no major changes should be expected, was soon replaced by an eerie silence. Their jilted left hander from the 2009 season, Cliff Lee, was out there on the open market, entertaining offers from the Texas Rangers and the New York Yankees. The Bronx Bombers had an offer on the table for six years and $150 million. Texas hoped to retain the southpaw, mortgaging seven years at $161 million in an effort to keep Lee. And while it was assumed that his future seemed certain to be in either Arlington or New York, reports of a different team entering the fray surfaced. Sadly, there was certainly no way that the surprise team in question could be the Phillies.

Well, the ensuing Big Bang resonated not just around the Delaware Valley, but throughout all of baseball. The weekly talk that Lee might actually return to Philadelphia in 2011 continued to surface on talk radio and from those supposedly "in the know." But few gave credence to those thoughts. After all, if

Shane Victorino takes part in sliding drills at the Phillies' spring training complex in February 2011.

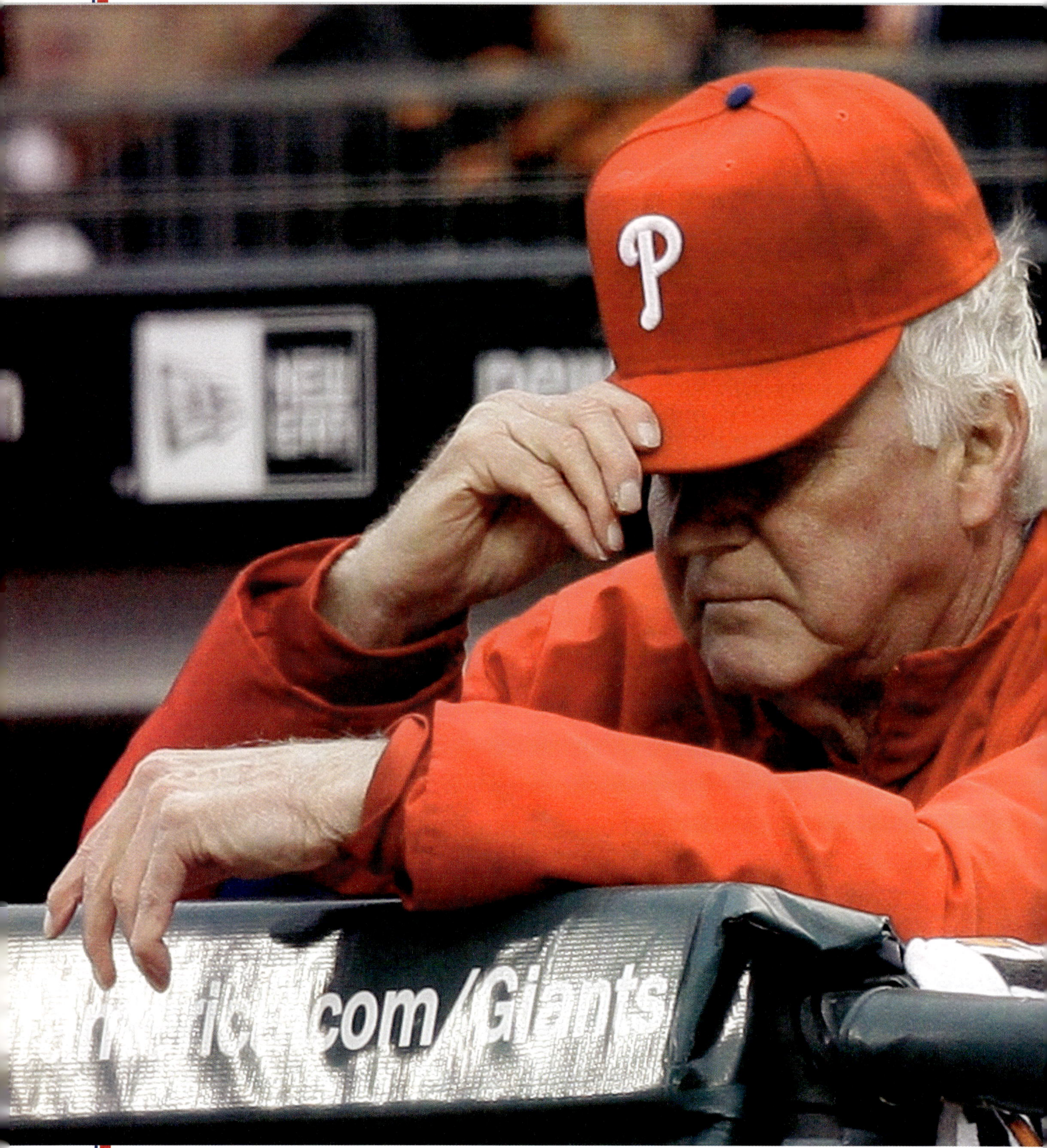
com/Giants

the Phillies were not able to afford to keep an offensive producer like Jayson Werth, there was simply no way that they would blow open the doors of their budget to pay uber-bucks to sign the talented lefty.

Guess again. Christmas came 11 days early in Philadelphia, as on December 14 it was announced that the team had indeed agreed to terms with Lee. His agreement to a five-year, $120 million contract gave the Phillies the best starting four in the game. But even more surprisingly refreshing was that with Cliff Lee, it wasn't all about the money. He signed with the Phillies for $41 million less than the Rangers' offer and $30 million less than the offer from New York.

"When you hit a certain point, enough is enough," he said. "It's just a matter of where you're comfortable, where you're happy and where your family is most comfortable and where you have the best chance to win.

"When you evaluate your options and get to pitch in a rotation with Halladay, Oswalt, and Hamels, that was all I needed to see right then. That was the major thing. To be in this rotation and be with this team was kind of a no-brainer for me."

So the best Fab Four in baseball will feature Roy Halladay, Cliff Lee, Roy Oswalt, and Cole Hamels, now known as R2C2 as the rotation includes two Roys, a Cole, and a Cliff. The fifth starter could be Blanton or Kendrick, barring a trade. And the bullpen continues to look good after closer Brad Lidge rebounded with a strong 2010 campaign. He'll be joined by setup man Ryan Madson, lefty specialist J.C. Romero, and Jose Contreras.

With the powerful starting lineup returning, sans Werth, 2011 promises to be a season of continued bangs in Philadelphia. For that to happen, the core players of the offense—Rollins, Utley, Victorino, and Howard—need to put up the kind of numbers they have done in the past. But based on their history and the addition of Lee to the starting rotation, the team is the odds-on favorite to win the division and go deep in the playoffs once again in 2011.

There is no doubt that the 2011 edition of the Philadelphia Phillies is blessed with some of the best pitching in the game and also boasts a pair of former Most Valuable Players in Howard and Rollins. Good pitching stops good hitting at least seven times out of 10, but will the pitching be the most important area on the team this year, or the ability to score runs?

"Well Charlie will tell you that we gotta score runs, plain and simple," said Moyer. "But I'm going to be biased here. If the pitchers do their job and the defense does its job, the hitting will be there but there just isn't quite as much pressure on them to perform. If you are giving up four and a half runs a game, think of what that means to your offense and what it needs to do for you to be successful.

"To me, it is pitching and defense that sets the tone of the game. If you can keep pitch counts down and show good defense to go with it, that's what keeps you in games and gives you a chance to win.

"If the pitchers do their job, that's where it all starts." ∎

Charlie Manuel watches from the AT&T Park dugout during the Phillies' Game 5 win over the Giants in the 2010 National League Championship Series.

Armed & Dangerous

2

R2C2 — Arms Control

The old baseball axiom that good pitching stops good hitting continues. It certainly proved true in last year's National League Championship Series when Tim Lincecum and Matt Cain paved the path for the San Francisco victory over the Phillies. Closer Brian Wilson gave the Giants a hammer at the back end of the bullpen who put the final nails in the Phillies' 2010 season. Even though 2010 has to be considered a successful season, the unexpected ouster at the hands of the Giants in the NLCS made the winter just a little bit colder for Phillies fans.

In 2010, Philadelphia ranked sixth in team ERA with a 3.67 mark. The staff ranked third in a comparison of playoff teams behind the Giants (3.36) and the Atlanta Braves (3.56). The starting rotation consisted of Roy Halladay, Cole Hamels, Joe Blanton, Jamie Moyer, and at times Kyle Kendrick and A.J. Happ. Strengthened by the mid-season acquisition of Roy Oswalt in a deal for Happ, the Phillies finished strong and overtook the Atlanta Braves during a September streak of effectiveness.

On the heels of a disappointing playoff loss at the hands of San Francisco, the Phillies' strongest team element just went from being very good to possibly the best in the game. The December signing of Cliff Lee, the prize free agent of this past off-season, gives Philadelphia as strong a rotation as there is in the game. Lee was 8–3 with Seattle before being sent to Texas where he pitched better than his 4–6 record indicates.

Halladay, Lee, Hamels, and Oswalt combined for a 52–31 record in 2010. Better things are expected in 2011. The fifth spot in the rotation could include holdovers Blanton and/or Kendrick.

Having such depth and talent in the starting rotation not only puts the rotation in an elite class, but has a trickle-down effect that could make the

Roy Halladay smiles alongside Cole Hamels (right) during an April 2010 game against the Giants.

Armed & Dangerous

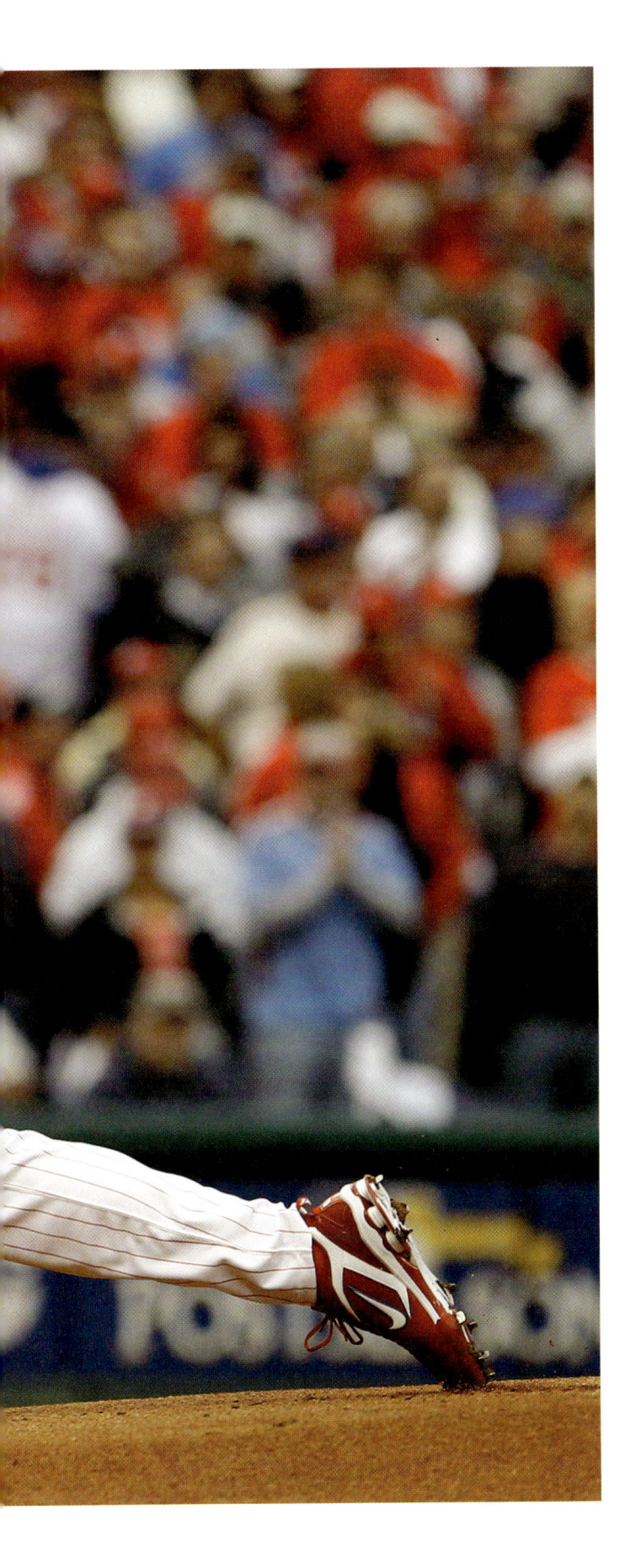

The 2011 Phillies: Perfectly Pitched & Poised to Dominate

bullpen much stronger as well. All of the components of a baseball team are connected to each other.

"Look at the history of those starters," Jamie Moyer said. "Adding the likes of Halladay, Oswalt, and Lee over the last two years is something that no general manager in the game would stick his nose up at. They still have to perform, but they are all professionals who have earned respect and earned responsibility.

"When I think about the dudes they have in the rotation, there is an added benefit in that it's going to take some of those meaningless innings away from the bullpen. The rotation as a whole will be pitching deeper into games, on average seven-plus innings a start. Now think about a bullpen that people used to say was a little short. What I think is going to happen is that as the rotation takes them deeper into games, the bullpen won't be called upon to pick up the fourth, fifth, or sixth innings, which will keep them sharper. Those meaningless innings take a toll. This starting rotation will keep the bullpen sharper by pitching deeper into games. So in effect, they have bettered their bullpen by adding more quality and depth to the rotation."

As the importance of pitching to postseason baseball glory cannot be denied, there is also no denying that the Phillies' staff is not just the best in baseball, but could be one of the best in the history of the game.

Only time will tell. And that time starts now. ■

Roy Halladay dominated the National League in 2010, winning the Cy Young Award with a 21–10 record and a 2.44 ERA.

ROY HALLADAY 34

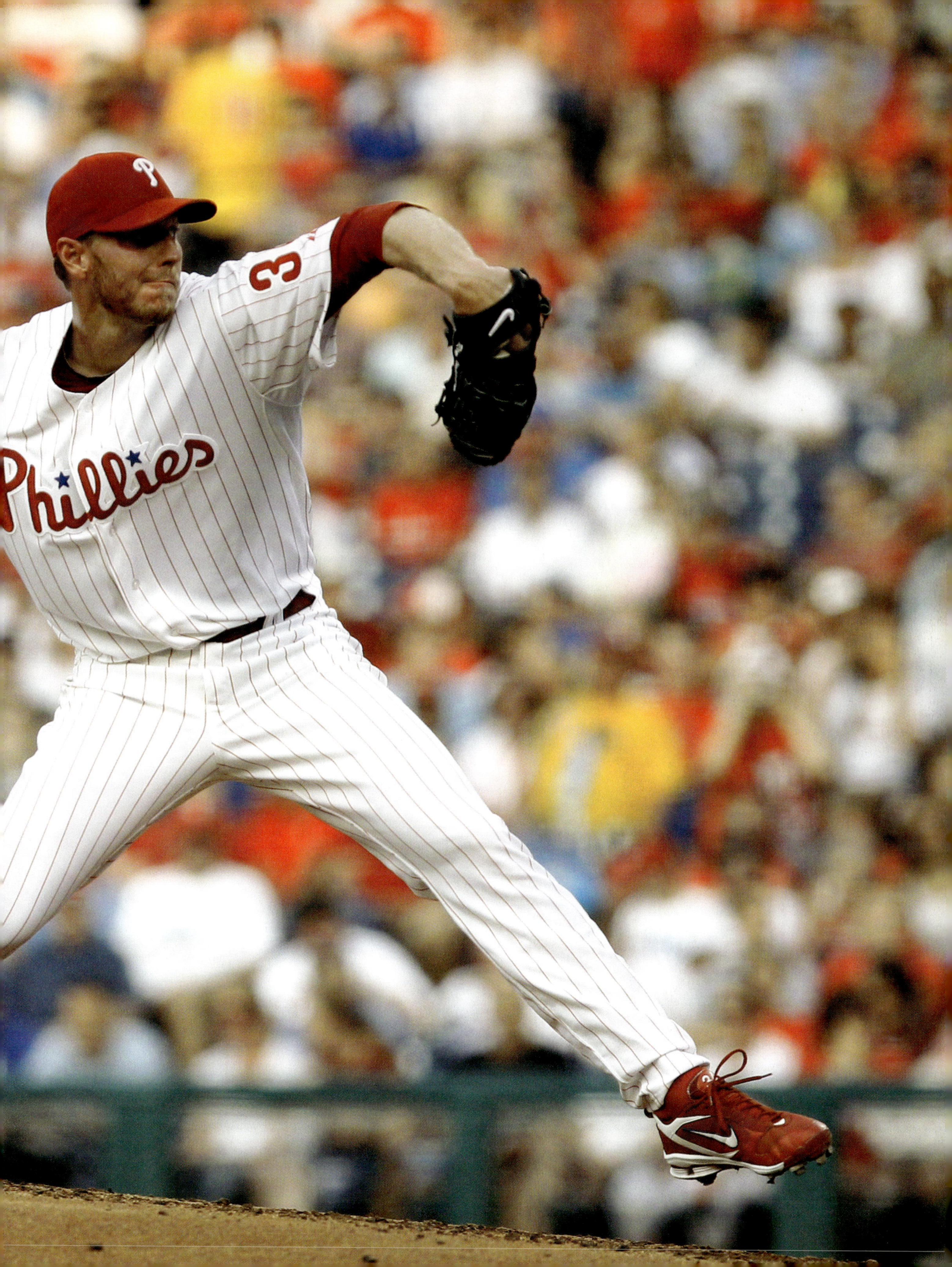
Phillies

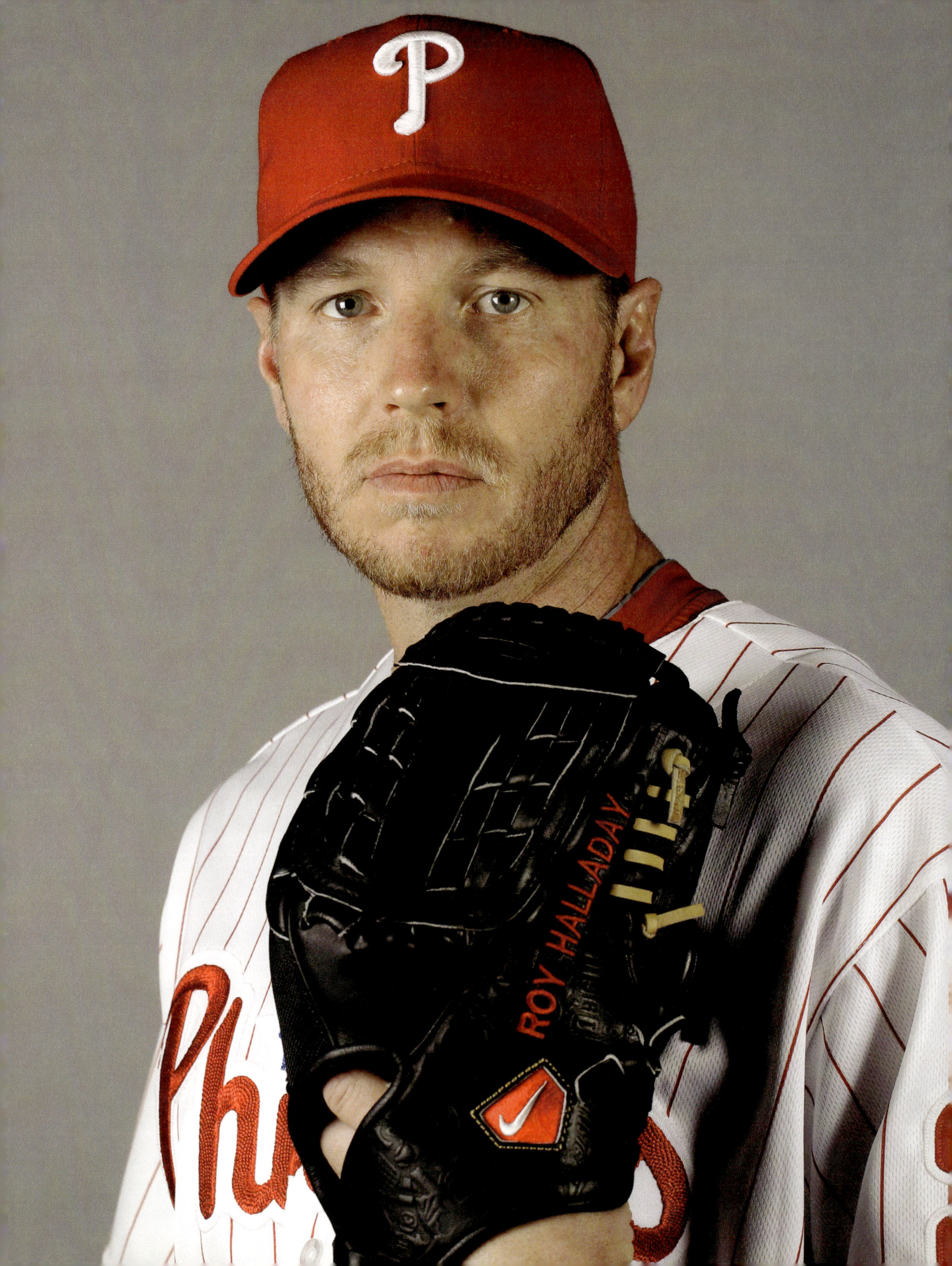
ROY HALLADAY

34
Roy Halladay

Born: May 14, 1977 | Ht: 6'6" | Wt: 230 lbs | B: R | T: R

	W-L	ERA	IP	Hits	BB	K	CG
2010:	21-10	2.44	250.2	231	30	219	9
Career:	169-86	3.32	2297.1	2228	485	1714	58

When former Toronto Blue Jays announcer Tom Cheeks christened Roy Halladay with the nickname Doc, it was a reference to the gunslinger from the Old West, "Doc" Holliday. Anyone who has seen the pitching "Doc" Halladay on the mound knows that the big right-hander surveys each hitter with steel gunslinger eyes and picks most opposing hitters apart like he was armed with a six-shooter. He is clearly a guy who does not give opposing hitters comfortable at-bats.

Halladay's 2010 statistics were impressive. In winning the National League Cy Young Award he became just the fifth pitcher to win that hallowed award in both leagues, joining Gaylord Perry, Pedro Martinez, Randy Johnson, and Roger Clemens. He led the National League in wins, innings pitched, complete games, and shutouts. Halladay also became the first pitcher to throw 250 or more innings and issue 30 or fewer walks since Grover Cleveland Alexander in 1927. It's also pretty difficult to forget the regular-season perfect game and the postseason no-hitter. Suffice to say that the Phillies have no regrets over the December 16, 2009 deal in which they acquired Halladay from the Blue Jays in exchange for Michael Taylor, Travis d'Arnaud, and Kyle Drabek.

And even though the Phillies came up short in the postseason loss to the San Francisco Giants, Halladay has no regrets about moving to the Phillies after a long and successful tenure in Toronto.

"The whole year was a dream come true for me," he said. "It's the most fun I've ever had. Of course it's a little bittersweet because we came up short of the goal we had as a team. But the stuff we all accomplished I'll never forget. It was everything I hoped it would be."

The ouster of the club was certainly not a positive but it may have had a silver lining that benefited both Halladay and the Phillies. The defeat at the hands of San Francisco kept Halladay from going out to the mound again with that injured groin, which could have resulted in a more serious injury. He fought through six

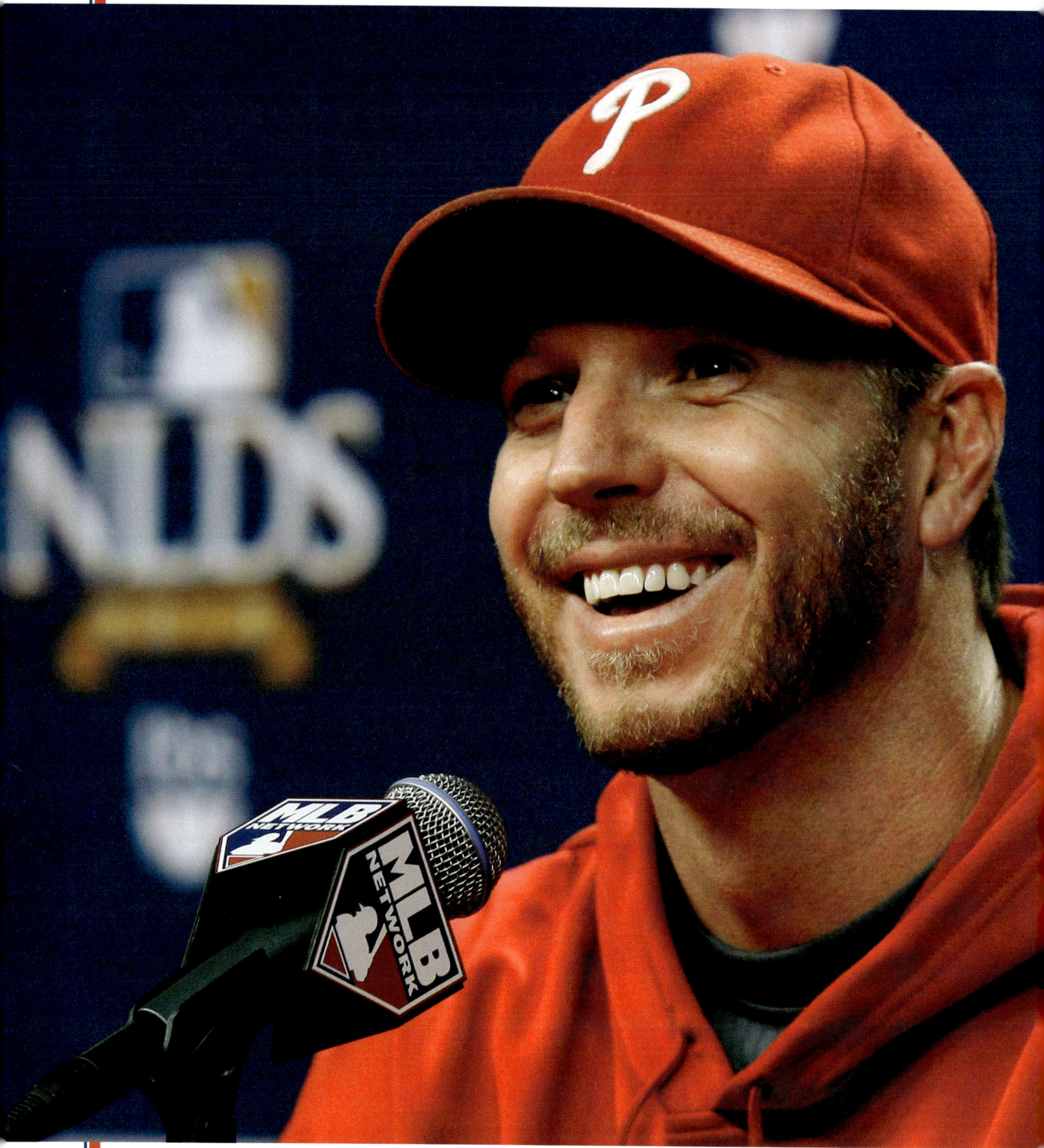
NLDS
MLB NETWORK
MLB NETWORK

tough innings in Game 6 of the Giants series and no doubt would have wanted the ball when his turn in the rotation came up again. The immediate rest helped the injury heal and he has updated his training regimen to include strengthening his lower body.

"After two weeks, I felt good and it was back into the regular off-season program," Halladay said. "It was completely gone as far as I could tell. We have added a lot of lower-half stuff to hopefully guard that area and make it a non-issue. I felt good after those two weeks. It's really completely gone as far as I can tell."

While he has had five stints on the disabled list in his 13 big-league seasons, he has always stepped up and pitched high numbers of quality innings. Breaking into The Show for the first time in 1998, he was a regular with the Blue Jays the following year with an 8–7 season. But he stumbled in 2000 with a disappointing 4–7 mark and an even more disturbing 10.64 ERA.

Halladay was dispatched to the minor leagues to open the 2001 season. But not just the minors, the low minors to Toronto's Class A team in Dunedin where he worked with the organizations pitching guru, Mel Queen. Although his velocity was in the mid-90s, Halladay's fastball was straight. Most major league hitters can adjust and handle a straight hummer even thrown harder than that.

Queen had him change his arm angle and his altered delivery resulted in a more deceptive motion and, more importantly, dramatic movement on his pitches. No longer throwing over the top in an overhand motion, Halladay now threw with a three-quarters delivery, between overhand and sidearm.

The results were immediate. In short order he was promoted to AA Tennessee and AAA Syracuse before being recalled to Toronto in mid-season where he

Roy Halladay was all smiles after starting the Phillies' 2010 postseason off with a no-hitter against the Cincinnati Reds.

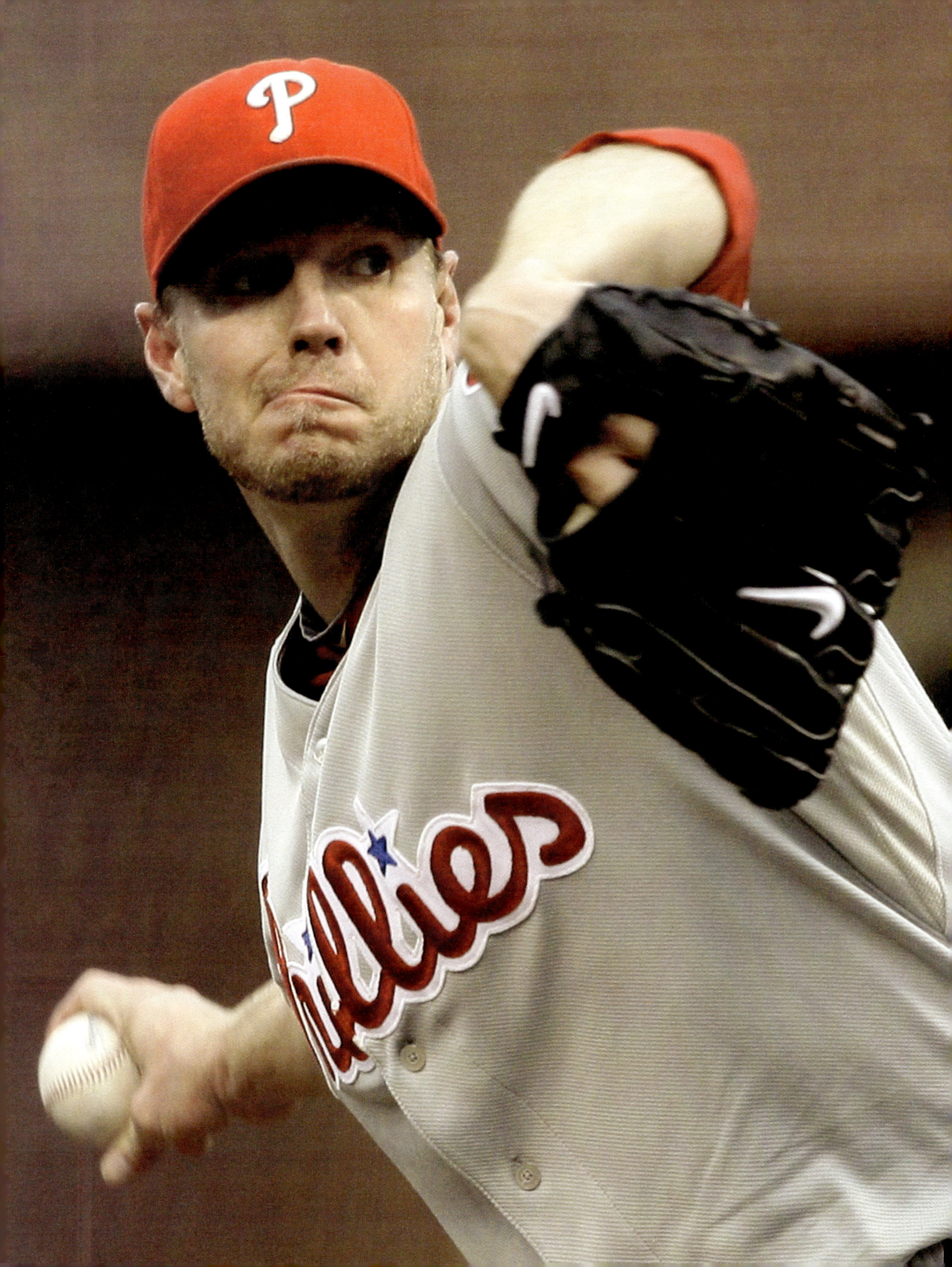

went 5–3 in 17 games. In 2002, Halladay had a breakout season, sporting a 19–7 record with a 2.93 ERA. He captured his first Cy Young Award in 2003 with a 22–7 mark and a 3.25 ERA in a season in which he led the league in wins, innings pitched (266), winning percentage (.759), and strikeouts (253).

He was just 8–8 the following season and landed on the disabled list on two occasions. But a 12–4 record in 2005, followed by a pair of 16-win seasons set the stage for Halladay's second 20-win campaign in 2008, when he had a 20–11 mark and a stellar 2.78 ERA.

Another outstanding 17–10 year in 2009 only cemented his place as one of the best pitchers in the game. At this point, he was also one of the most sought-after pitchers in the league. Although he loved pitching in Toronto, he yearned to play for a contender, which led to the trade to the Phillies. He seems incredibly happy and in good physical condition following the playoff groin injury last fall.

"What you see is what you get with Roy," said Jamie Moyer. "He's a very quiet guy who comes to work with his lunch pail. It's all business for Roy. Very seldom do you see him just sitting at his locker doing nothing. I liken him to Chase Utley in that regard. When you see guys like that it creates more of a responsibility for everyone to be prepared for your job. What Roy does on the field speaks for itself. Like Chase, he is a no-nonsense guy who works diligently to make himself the best player he can be and also the best teammate he can be. They lead by example and it rubs off on a lot of the other players."

A healthy Halladay certainly speaks volumes for the front of the Phillies' rotation. The addition of Cliff Lee to the other ace holdovers, Cole Hamels and Roy Oswalt, gives this team as strong a rotation as there is in the game today. If they all stay healthy and pitch up to their capabilities, opposing teams will find this a very difficult season.

But as has been repeated many times during the winter, the goal is not just to throw good statistics out there. The ultimate goal is the win the World Series, and Roy Halladay is not just an overpowering pitcher, but a real leader on and off the diamond who helps the team stay focused on that ultimate goal.

"He is a very good guy and a very good person," said Chris Wheeler. "He's the same guy every day, except for the days he pitches. Roy is one of the greatest competitors I've ever seen. He maxes out with all the preparation and is ready to go in every game he pitches. With him, every pitch out there is a war. Every pitch out there means something to him. Sometimes he gets ticked off at umpires when he doesn't get a pitch that he wants because he is trying to set something up.

"Every pitch is so important to him, the whole idea of setting up the hitter. It's like Tim McCarver used to say, it's how you get there and he gets there by setting guys up."

It will not be easy for Roy Halladay to match the season he had in 2010. But if preparation, determination, and ability mean anything, he may have to make space on his mantel for some new awards...perhaps another Cy Young Award, and hopefully a World Series ring. ∎

Acquired from Toronto after the 2009 season, two-time Cy Young Award winner Roy Halladay leads a rotation that includes four former All-Stars and three former 20-game winners.

CLIFF LEE

33

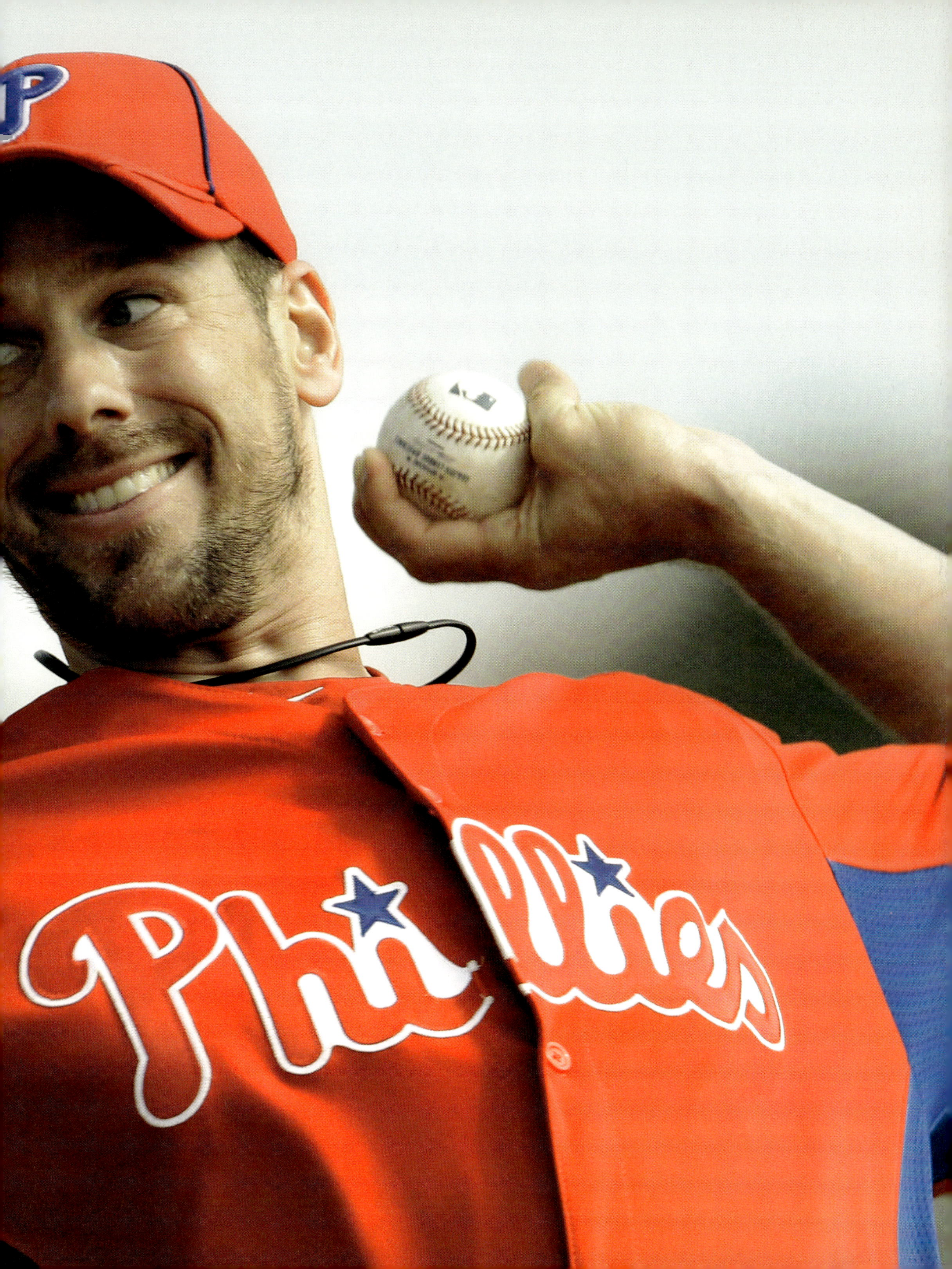
Phillies

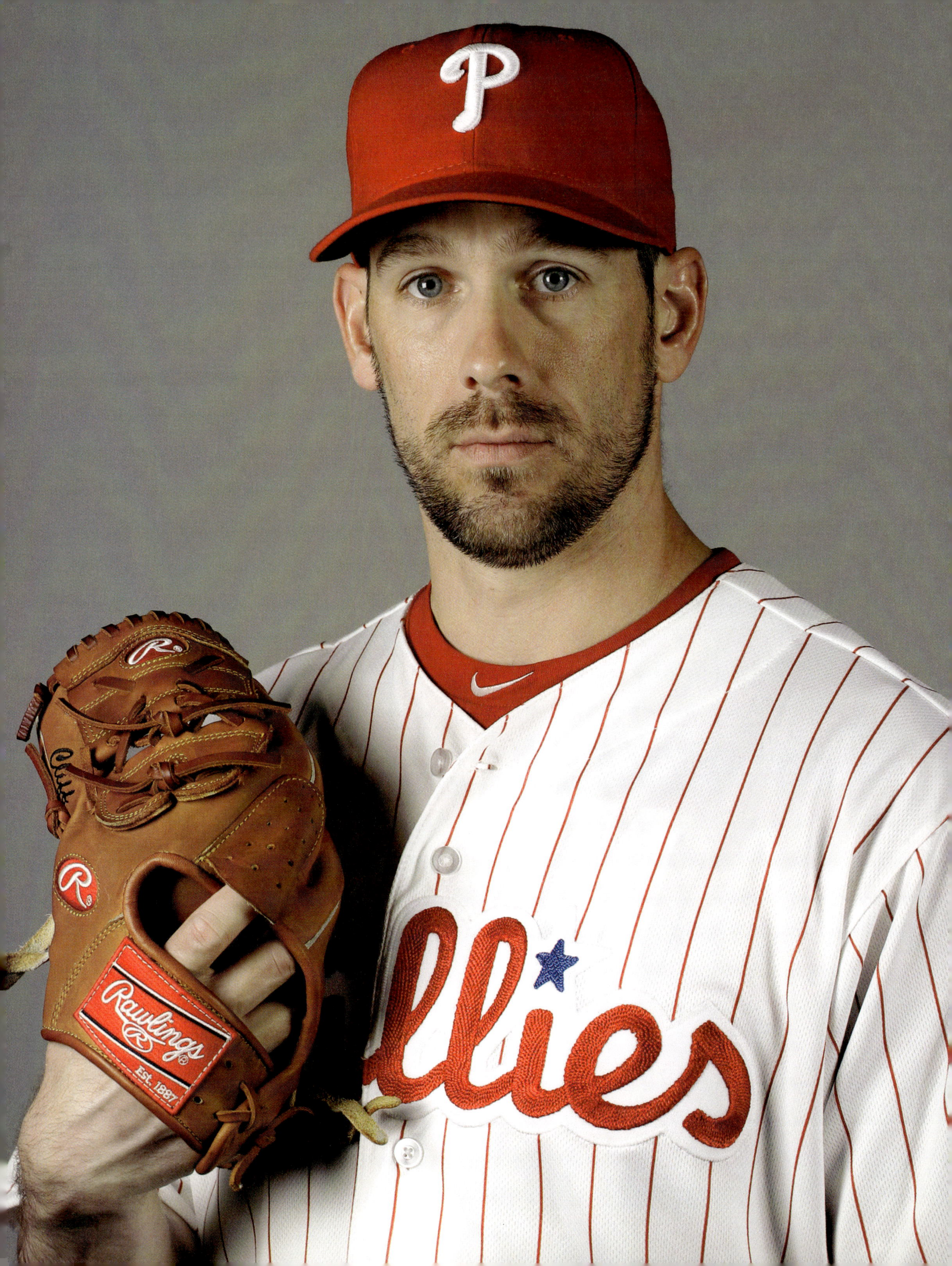
Rawlings
Est. 1887
llies

33
Cliff Lee

Born: August 30, 1978 | Ht: 6'3" | Wt: 190 lbs | B: L | T: L

	W–L	ERA	IP	Hits	BB	K	CG
2010:	12–9	3.18	212.1	195	18	185	7
Career:	102–61	3.85	1409	1419	350	1085	20

For a while, it seemed as though Cliff Lee was going to be one of those hired guns. A baseball player who would be traded time and again from a downtrending team to a midseason contender. After all, it was happening with maddening regularity.

In his eighth year with the Cleveland Indians, following a splendid 22–3 season in 2008 with a 2.54 ERA, Lee was dealt to the reigning World Series champion Phillies on July 29. The stylish southpaw responded with a 7–4 mark down the stretch and a resounding 4–0 postseason record. But with the acquisition of Roy Halladay on the horizon at the cost of some top-notch minor league prospects, the team chose to send Lee to the Seattle Mariners for a trio of highly-rated prospects to replace those sent to Toronto for Halladay.

Lee and an entire Phillies fan base were aghast at the turn of events. But that disappointment didn't keep Lee from pitching well with the Mariners, where he went 8–3 with a 2.34 ERA. Seattle was out of playoff contention and in early July traded him to the contending Texas Rangers for four prospects. While he went only 4–6 with Texas the remainder of the regular season, Lee was 3–0 in the postseason and helped lead the Rangers to the World Series against San Francisco.

"Cliff is very much like Roy," said his former teammate Moyer. "He is a professional who is deliberate about what he is doing and is a great competitor who doesn't like to get beat. He is so focused on who he is as a pitcher and what he has. He has such confidence in every pitch he has. He is the kind of guy who might not throw his curveball for two innings and then throw it with two strikes on a guy. When you can use all your pitches on both sides of the plate like Cliff, it is very, very difficult to hit."

As has been documented many times, to the surprise of just about everyone who was not involved in the negotiations, Lee spurned more lucrative offers from Texas and the New York Yankees to return to Philadelphia, where he never wanted to leave in the first place. Baseball's traveling man had found a home.

"I enjoyed my time in Seattle," Lee said after inking his deal in Philadelphia. "I enjoyed my time in

Armed & Dangerous

The 2011 Phillies: Perfectly Pitched & Poised to Dominate

Texas. Looking back, I'm kind of glad I had the chance to go back to the World Series. I had a great time in Texas and I got to play close to home. But now I'm back here and I'm looking forward to it.

"It's great to land back here in Philadelphia, where I never wanted to leave in the first place. From the moment I got here, the first day, I knew it was something special."

Lee first pitched in the major leagues in parts of 2002 and 2003 with the Cleveland Indians and had a combined 3–4 record. He became a full timer in 2004 with a 14–8 record, followed by an 18–5 mark the following year and a 14–11 record in 2006. But 2007 did not start out well for the lanky lefty. It also didn't end well, and was not pretty in between.

(opposite and above) Cliff Lee takes part in spring training workouts at the Phillies' facility in Clearwater, Florida, in mid-March, 2011. Lee, who pitched for the National League champion Phillies in 2009, returned to Philadelphia as a free agent after pitching for the Seattle Mariners and Texas Rangers in 2010.

Armed & Dangerous

A strained groin saw him start the season on the disabled list. When he did come back he was not the same pitcher and was sent packing to AAA. After three consecutive winning seasons, Cliff Lee stumbled to 5–8 record in 2007. But he bounced back with a vengeance the following year, earning the American League Cy Young Award with a 22–3 record and a 2.54 ERA.

He pitched well in 2009 for the Indians with a 7–9 record and an ERA of 3.14. But the trade winds were blowing and Lee was sent to the Phillies along with outfielder Ben Francisco on July 29 for a package of prospects.

All Lee did with the Phillies was finish the regular season with a fine 7–4 record and a 3.39 ERA. But it's what he did in the postseason that made him the stuff of legend in the City of Brotherly Love. He was 1–0, 1.10 ERA in the NLDS, 1–0, 0.00 in the NLCS, and 2–0, 2.81 in the World Series against the powerful New York Yankees. Talk about money in the bank.

Imagine the shockwaves that were felt when he was sent packing to Seattle that December in exchange for prospects. He thought he had found a home in Philadelphia and was hoping to work out a long-term contract. Fans were sick and he was clearly disappointed.

His time as a member of the Phillies was pretty special for the locals as well, who considered him not just an outstanding pitcher but one of the real nice guys of the game as well. The question that haunted the organization was why not keep both Halladay and Lee? Almost as unsatisfactory as the trading of Lee to Seattle was the team's explanation that they needed to replace the prospects lost in the Halladay deal.

While the team's new ace certainly won over the fan base, Jamie Moyer, Joe Blanton, and Kyle Kendrick took the mound and gave the Phillies quality games and innings. But often during the season, the familiar cry about not keeping Lee would surface. And like his pitching partner Halladay, Lee also brings as much to the clubhouse as he does the pitching mound.

"He is just a good guy who is very personable," said Chris Wheeler. "Here's another guy who is always prepared and has an approach when he goes out there. Even when he gets his butt kicked, it's not the end of the world. He is a location guy, not a blow them away guy. He's very professional about the way he goes about pitching."

For more than a year it seemed as if Roy Halladay and Cliff Lee simply would not work out in Philadelphia. At the end of the day, the business side of baseball precluded that from happening. But General Manager Ruben Amaro Jr. and the front office did some magic with the team budget and now the two erstwhile aces are finally together.

Teamed with Halladay, Cliff Lee gives the Phillies as good a one-two punch as there is in the game. And happily for Philadelphia fans, it doesn't end there! ■

Akron Aeros pitcher Cliff Lee throws in the Double A All-Star Game on July 10, 2002. A few weeks earlier, the Cleveland Indians acquired Lee from the Montreal Expos as part of a trade that moved All-Star pitcher Bartolo Colon to Montreal. Lee made his major league debut with the Indians later that season.

COLE HAMELS

35

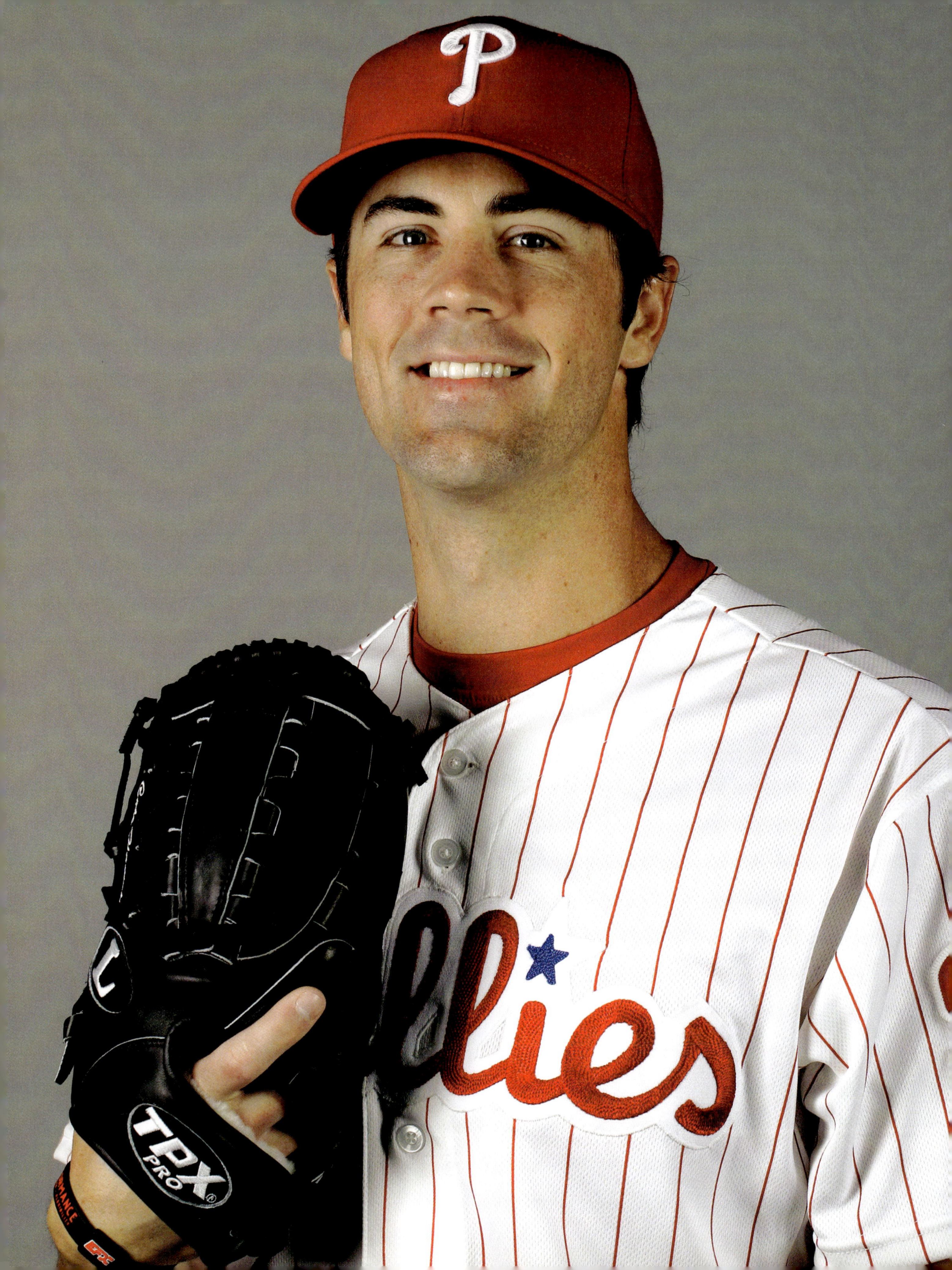
TPX
PRO

35
Cole Hamels

	W-L	ERA	IP	Hits	BB	K	CG
2010:	12-11	3.06	208.2	185	61	211	1
Career:	60-45	3.53	945.1	864	248	897	7

Born: December 27, 1983 | Ht: 6'4" | Wt: 190 lbs | B: L | T: L

The only member of R2C2 to come out of the Phillies' farm system, Cole Hamels was the team's first round pick in the 2002 draft, and the 17th player chosen overall. After a quick rise through the Phillies' farm system, not without some pratfalls, the lanky lefty first made it to The Show in 2006. Just two years later, he was named Most Valuable Player of the National League Championship Series as well as the World Series. Not a bad couple of years.

After breaking into to professional baseball with a bang in 2003, going a combined 6–3 for Clearwater and Lakewood, Hamels injured his elbow in 2004 and was limited to just four games. Youth was served prior to the 2005 campaign when the young prospect broke his pitching hand in a bar brawl prior to spring training. After recovering from that incident he then injured his back, which limited him to six appearances, four of which were wins.

Back healthy and determined in 2006, Hamels was promoted to Philadelphia in early May after hitters in Lakewood, Clearwater, and Scranton/Wilkes Barre were not even competitive. Hamels went 9–8 with Philadelphia that season with a 4.08 ERA. He was young but he was also one of the most talented pitchers to come out of the Phillies' farm system in years.

Hamels really came of age in 2007, going 15–5 with a 3.39 ERA and helping the Phillies win the Eastern Division crown. Although they were swept in the NLDS by Colorado, this team's potential was off the charts. And Hamels' high ceiling was obvious to all. Gifted with a fastball in the mid-90s, he also features a cut fastball, hard-breaking curve, and one of the best change-ups in the game. He also has one of those great California personalities that people love to be around.

"To me, Cole Hamels is one of the more misunderstood guys in this town because people think he's soft because he's a good looking guy," said Chris Wheeler. "But he is so mentally tough, which people don't see. He is very, very tough on himself. He and Rich Dubee

Armed & Dangerous

The 2011 Phillies: Perfectly Pitched & Poised to Dominate

(Phillies pitching coach) were working on some different approaches, he got his fastball back last year because he was healthy and he also stopped beating himself up when things went wrong. He wants to win as much as anybody out there and is immensely talented. He's just better than most people and he just loves the game. He loves to pitch, field, hit, work on his move to first base. He is just a hard working kid who to me is very special."

There are many words to describe the 2008 season for the Philadelphia Phillies and special is certainly one of them. It was the year in which they ended a 28-year drought between sips from baseball's championship fountain. And one of the mainstays of that team was Cole Hamels.

(left) Teammates shower Cole Hamels in champagne after Hamels pitched a complete-game shutout to clinch the 2010 National League Division Series. **(above)** Hamels delivers a pitch during the Phillies' February 26 spring training game against the New York Yankees.

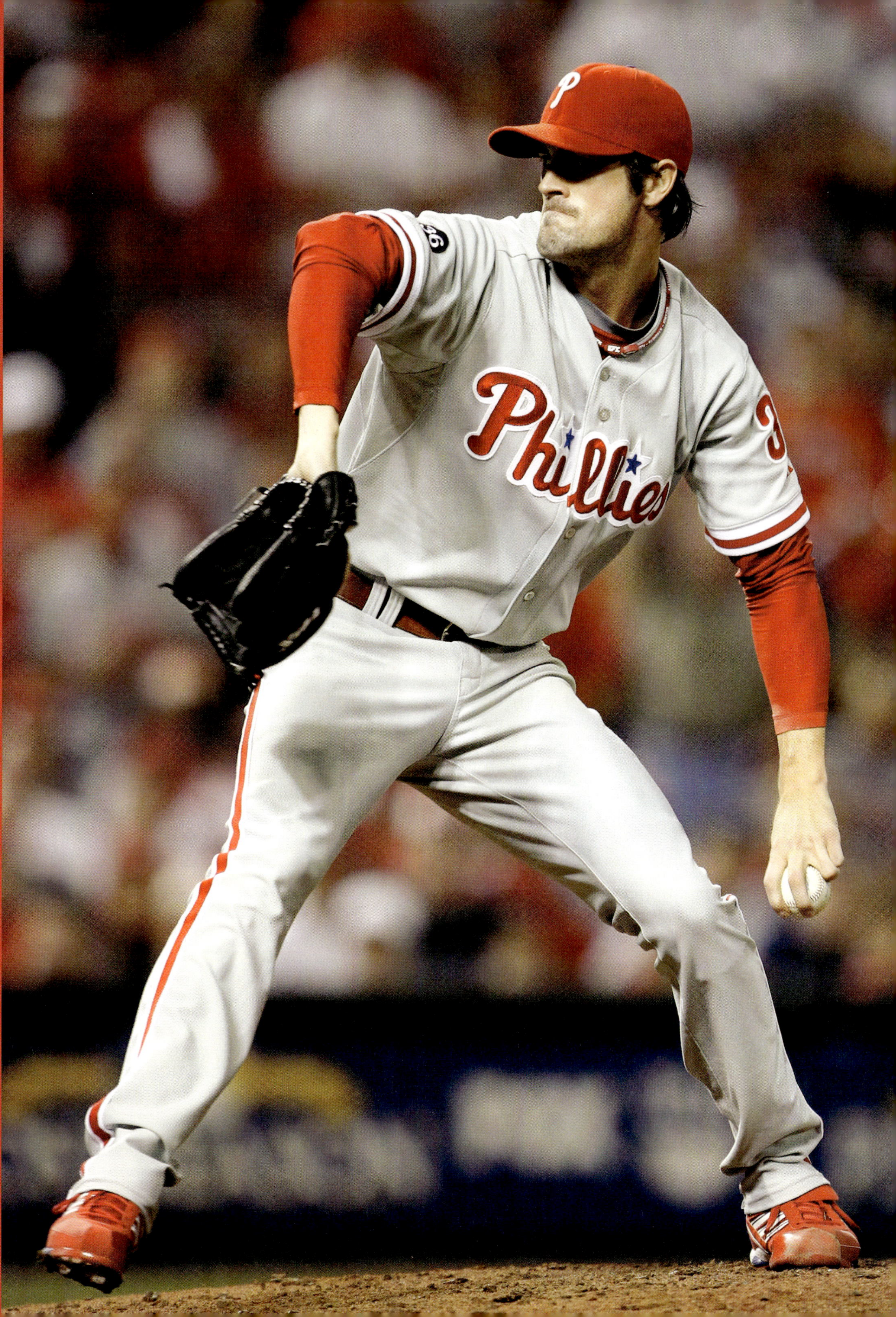
Phillies

After getting off to a bit of a troubling start when he expressed his unhappiness with his contract negotiations, he became one of the best pitchers in the game. The ace of the Phillies' staff, Hamels went 14–10 with a pair of shutouts and a 3.09 ERA. In 227 innings, he yielded just 193 hits, walked 53, and fanned 196 hitters. While his record was impressive enough, during much of the regular season Hamels was the guy who got the least amount of offensive support. He pitched well enough to have easily had an 18-win season.

Hamels is already an outstanding pitcher, but Jamie Moyer feels that he is still getting better and learning his craft.

"To me, Cole is still growing as a pitcher and I mean that in a very positive way," he said. "He is still learning about himself. One year he was the MVP in the playoffs and the next year he wasn't quite the same guy. That's what baseball is all about, dealing with your failures and inconsistency. He has learned a lot in that regard. He competes and is still fine-tuning his pitches. That's where he is growing greatly.

"He has also grown greatly in the competitive area and his focus has totally changed from when I first came over to the Phillies. Sometimes it's the things within that get you there. Those inner challenges of when you challenge yourself and you grow and learn. Cole has gained a great deal of confidence in his own ability."

The following season saw the Phillies once again earn division and league honors, returning to the Fall Classic but losing to the New York Yankees. Hamels wasn't quite as effective, as his 10–11 record and career high 4.32 ERA indicates. But he continued to grow and mature as a pitcher and a person and enjoyed his second consecutive injury-free season.

While his record in 2010 was 12–11, he was a much better pitcher with an ERA of 3.06. The addition of Halladay and Oswalt along with the return of Cliff Lee in 2011 should allow Hamels to concentrate on continuing to improve and consistently being the dominating pitcher the organization has seen so often.

It's shaping up to be another great season in Philadelphia, with hope for even more baseball history to be made. Hamels has been healthy and has become one of the elite pitchers in the game. And if he didn't need any more motivation, 2011 is the final year of his contract, which should add plenty of fuel to his fire. ■

The youngest of the Phillies four star starting pitchers at just 27, Cole Hamels enters the 2011 season with 60 career wins.

ROY OSWALT 44

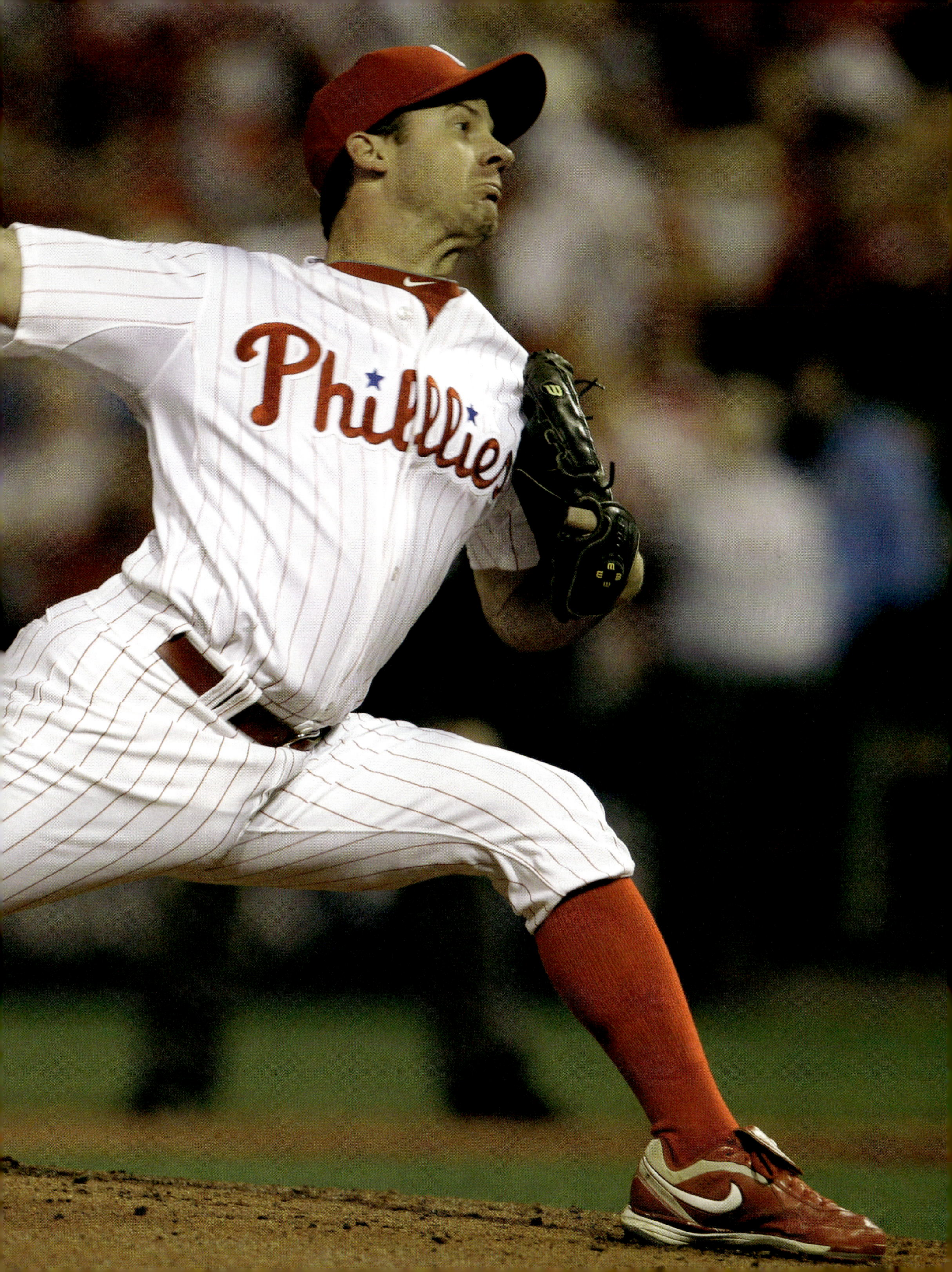
Phillies

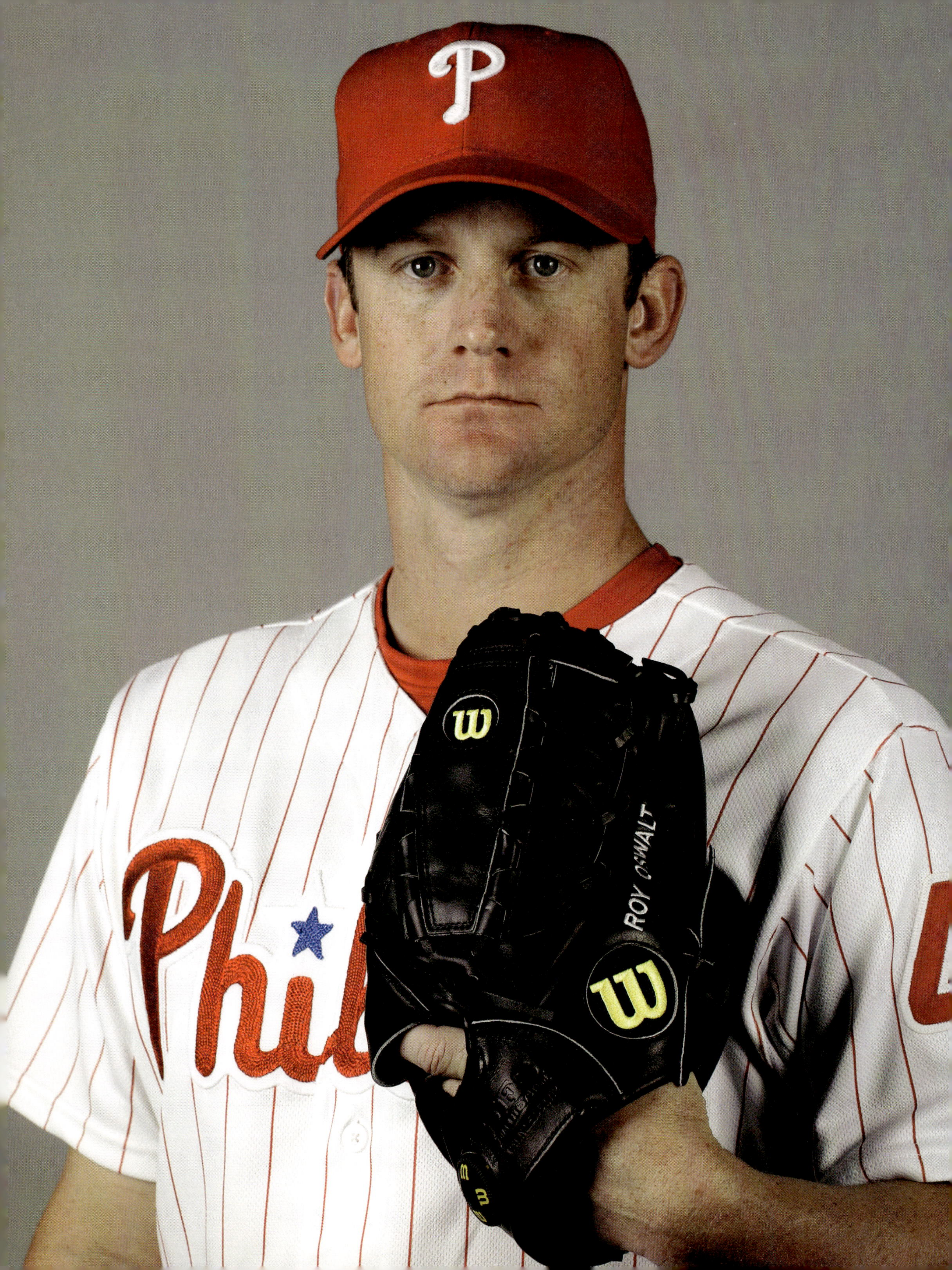
ROY OSWALT

44
Roy Oswalt

	W–L	ERA	IP	Hits	BB	K	CG
Born: August 29, 1977	**Ht: 6'0"**	**Wt: 185 lbs**	**B: R**	**T:R**			
2010:	13–13	2.76	211.2	162	55	193	2
Career:	150–83	3.18	2015	1918	467	1,666	20

Roy Oswalt is a very competitive man. He spent the first nine years of his big-league career with the Houston Astros, but as the organization continued in its rebuilding effort, it became more and more apparent that Oswalt's time with the club was coming to an end. A talented, determined, and professional pitcher in every way, the veteran right-hander's abilities were not being fully utilized in Houston. So when he was sent to the Phillies last July 29 in exchange for pitcher J.A. Happ, outfielder Anthony Gose, and shortstop Jonathan Villar, it must have seemed like a reprieve from the governor.

While that may be a bit of an overstatement, Oswalt was clearly ready to move on to a place that afforded him a chance to play on a contending team again and also helped the Astros build for a brighter future.

"I'm glad it worked out for both of us," Oswalt said of the trade. "I wanted to go to a contender and Houston gets some good prospects in return who will hopefully allow them to build a winning team. I've been in the same place for 10 years and having to say good-bye and clean out the locker was the toughest part."

After starting out the 2010 season with Houston, Oswalt had a 6–12 record with a more-than-respectable ERA of 3.42. But his presence in the rotation helped propel the Phillies into first place as he went 7–1 with a 1.74 ERA for Philadelphia following the trade. He also made some organizational history on August 24 against his former team when he became the first Phillies pitcher since Bill Wilson on August 6, 1971, to play a position other than pitcher. After Ryan Howard was ejected from a game against the Astros in the 14th inning, Raul Ibanez moved from left field to first base. Since the Phillies were out of position players, Oswalt came in to play left field and actually made a putout on a fly ball.

Armed & Dangerous

But his value to the team is clearly on the pitching mound. Still throwing a mid-90s fastball, Oswalt is a complete pitcher who also has an overhand curve, slider, and Vulcan change in his repertoire. He has good control and is an aggressive pitcher who goes after hitters with lots of fastballs, which only make his off-speed offerings even more effective. He plays hardball and makes things uncomfortable for opposing hitters.

"He is really competitive," said Chris Wheeler. "I have never heard of one hitter say that they wanted to face Oswalt. He'd knock his mother down. His change-up is really good. Although he won't go deep into games

Roy Oswalt joined the Phillies in July 2010 after spending 10 seasons with the Houston Astros. Oswalt's 7–1 record in 12 starts with the Phillies was key to Philadelphia's National League East title.

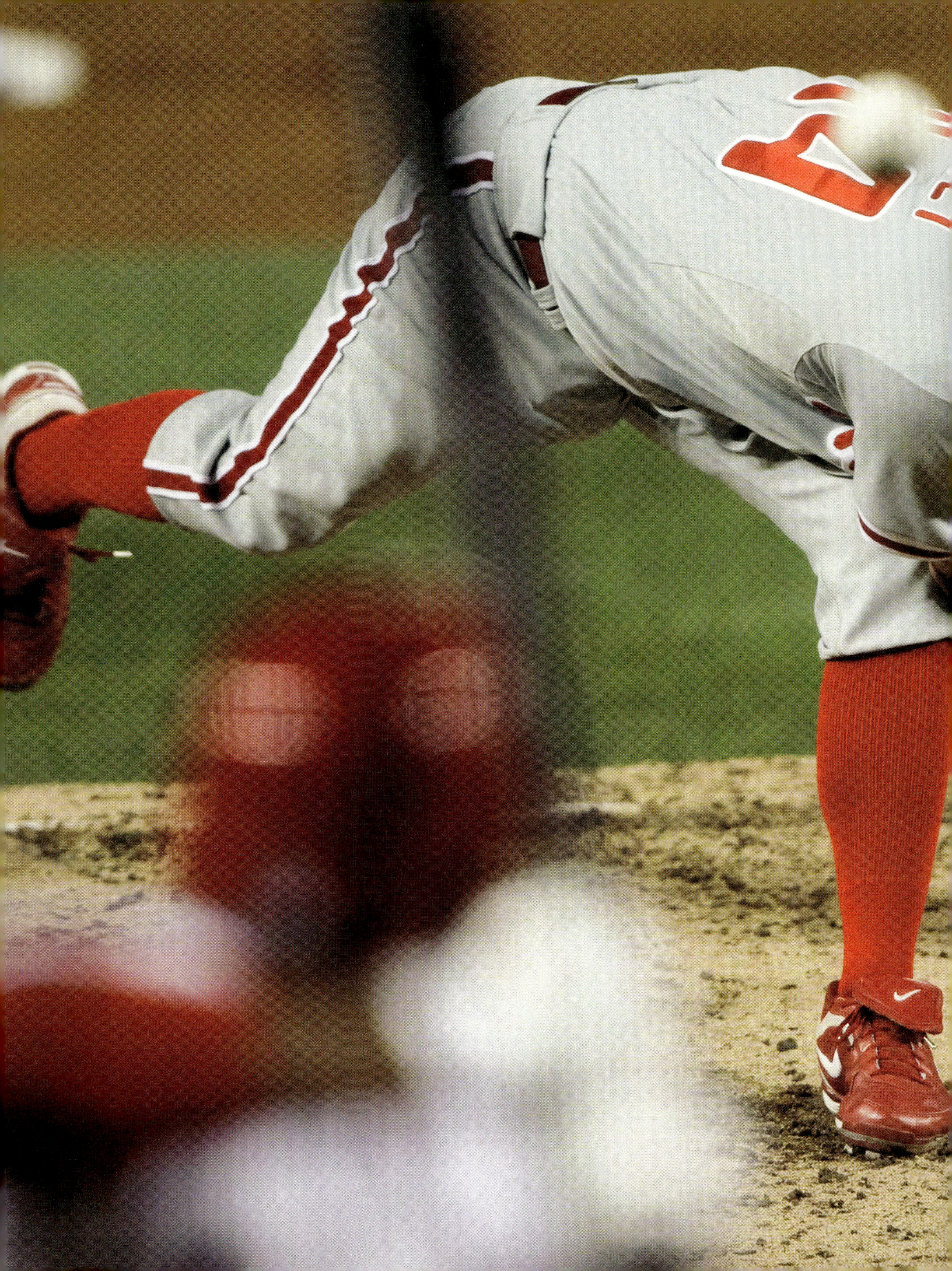

The 2011 Phillies: Perfectly Pitched & Poised to Dominate

as often as before because he's not a big guy, he is dead serious out there and a hell of an athlete. Roy is an immensely confident guy who is a delight to be around. And pound for pound, he is as tough as they go."

Oswalt was originally drafted by Houston in the 23rd round of the 1996 amateur draft. While making a steady climb through the Astros' farm system, a freak accident may have helped the young pitcher achieve his potential. While pitching for Michigan in the Midwest League in 1999, Oswalt was suffering from pain in his pitching shoulder that was causing much concern. As he was checking the spark plug wires in his truck, touching one of the wires caused the vehicle's engine to start, sending an electric current flowing through his body. After holding onto the spark plug for nearly a minute his foot slipped and he was finally thrown off the truck. But it is believed that the electric current actually loosened scar tissue in his sore shoulder, which has enabled him to pitch pain-free ever since.

Oswalt went 13–4 that season and a combined 15–7 in 2000, pitching for Kissimmee and Round Rock. He was Houston-bound the following season with a 14–3 record. He was a mainstay of the Houston staff averaging 15 wins per season, include 20-win seasons in 2004 and 2005.

But as Houston fell out of contention after having been a playoff team both of those seasons (including a World Series appearance in 2005), the look of the future there made the present in Philadelphia much brighter with the addition of Roy Oswalt to the rotation. ∎

Oswalt's success after joining the Phillies continued into the postseason. The Phillies won two of Oswalt's three postseason starts.

JOE BLANTON

56

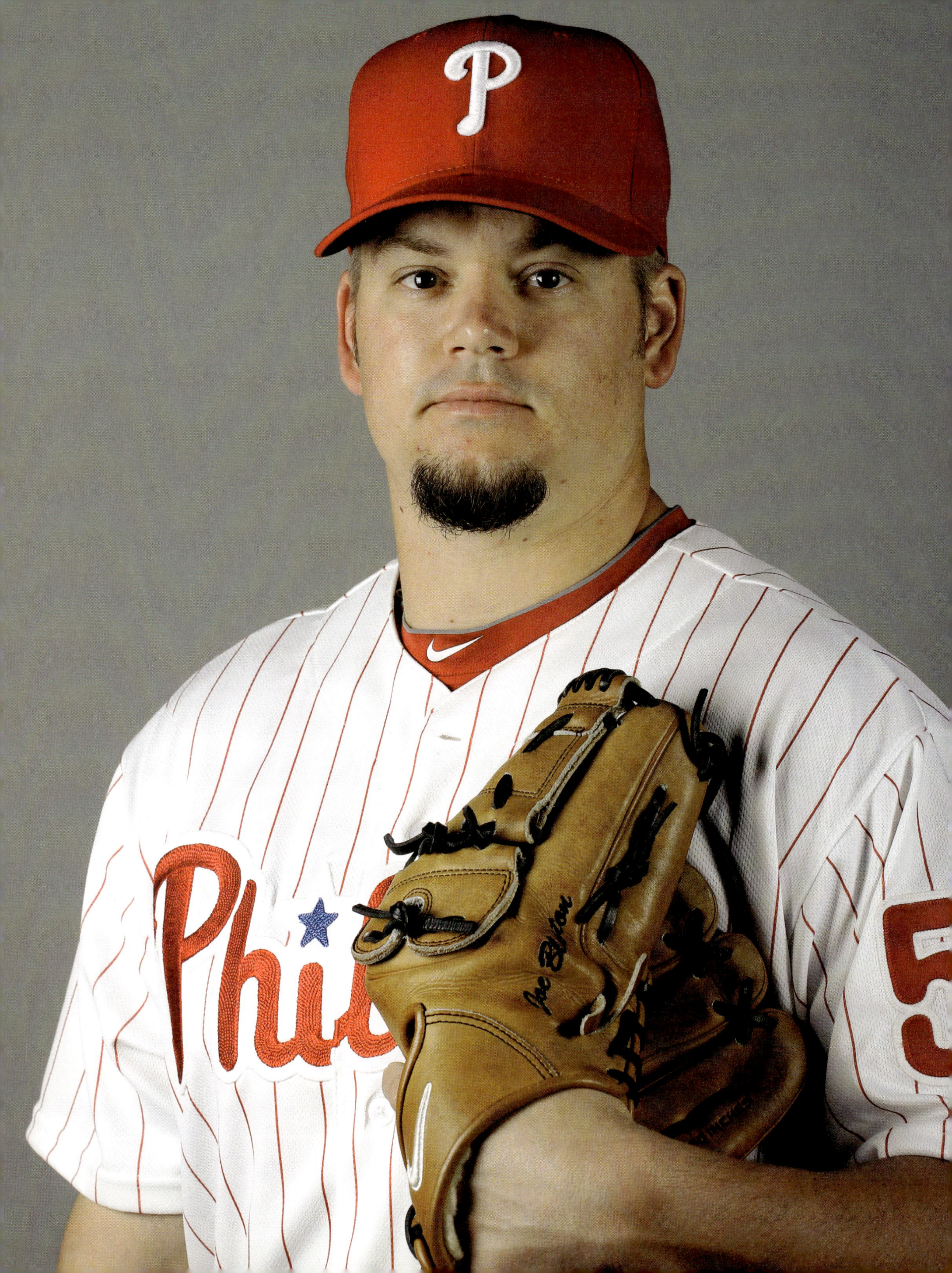

56 Joe Blanton

	Born: December 11, 1980	Ht: 6'3"	Wt: 245 lbs	B: R	T: R	
	W-L	ERA	IP	Hits	BB	K	CG
2010:	9-6	4.82	175.2	206	43	134	0
Career:	72-60	4.30	1202.1	1280	335	777	6

There is no doubt that the Phillies' starting rotation is filled with stars. R2C2, the Fab Four, and Four-of-a-Kind are nicknames that have been bandied about for Halladay, Lee, Hamels, and Oswalt. But while all are legitimate stars, there is a fifth member of the rotation who seems to be the forgotten man. Big Joe Blanton is clearly the Rodney Dangerfield of the Phillies' staff—the guy who simply gets no respect.

All Blanton has done in his career is be the dependable guy who goes out there every fifth day and gives his team a chance to win. An inning eater, he's averaged 6.3 innings per start in his big-league career. He could be the guy who quietly goes under the radar and adds 12 to 15 wins in 2011.

"I'm not big on attention," he said at the start of spring training. "And I don't think these other four guys are either. It doesn't matter to me. Winning is the biggest part for me."

After being acquired from the Oakland A's in 2008, Big Joe went 4–0 for the Phillies and helped them win their first World Series championship since 1980. He went 12–8 the following year and rebounded from an early season oblique injury that landed him on the disabled list to go 9–6 in 2010. After a rough start following his return from the disabled list, Blanton had a stretch in which he went 8–1. When Big Joe came back healthy, he did an outstanding job.

In his three full seasons with the A's, Blanton won 12, 16, and 14 games. He is clearly a guy who goes out to the mound and gives the team a chance to win. Consistency is the biggest part of his game.

Since the acquisition of Cliff Lee during the off-season, rumors have swirled about the team possibly trading Blanton to acquire a more veteran presence to replace Jayson Werth in right field. Kyle Kendrick and Vance Worley could possibly fill his spot in the rotation. A veteran pitcher, Blanton knows that trades are a part of the game. But as far as he is concerned, he hopes the Phillies keep him right where he is.

"You can't really think about that," he said. "All I'm

Armed & Dangerous

worried about is going out and trying to win another World Series with Philadelphia. I can't worry about the other part. That is the business part. That is what the people upstairs are for and they handle that. I love it here. I hope to stay here."

Joe Blanton is a luxury for an already flush Phillies team. He represents a strong and solid fifth starter in the best rotation in the game.

Big Joe might be the Rodney Dangerfield of the Phillies' rotation, but his teammates and opponents both know what a valuable member of this pitching staff he is. ∎

The forgotten man in the Phillies' 2011 starting rotation is Joe Blanton, who has recorded 12 or more wins in four of his seven big-league seasons.

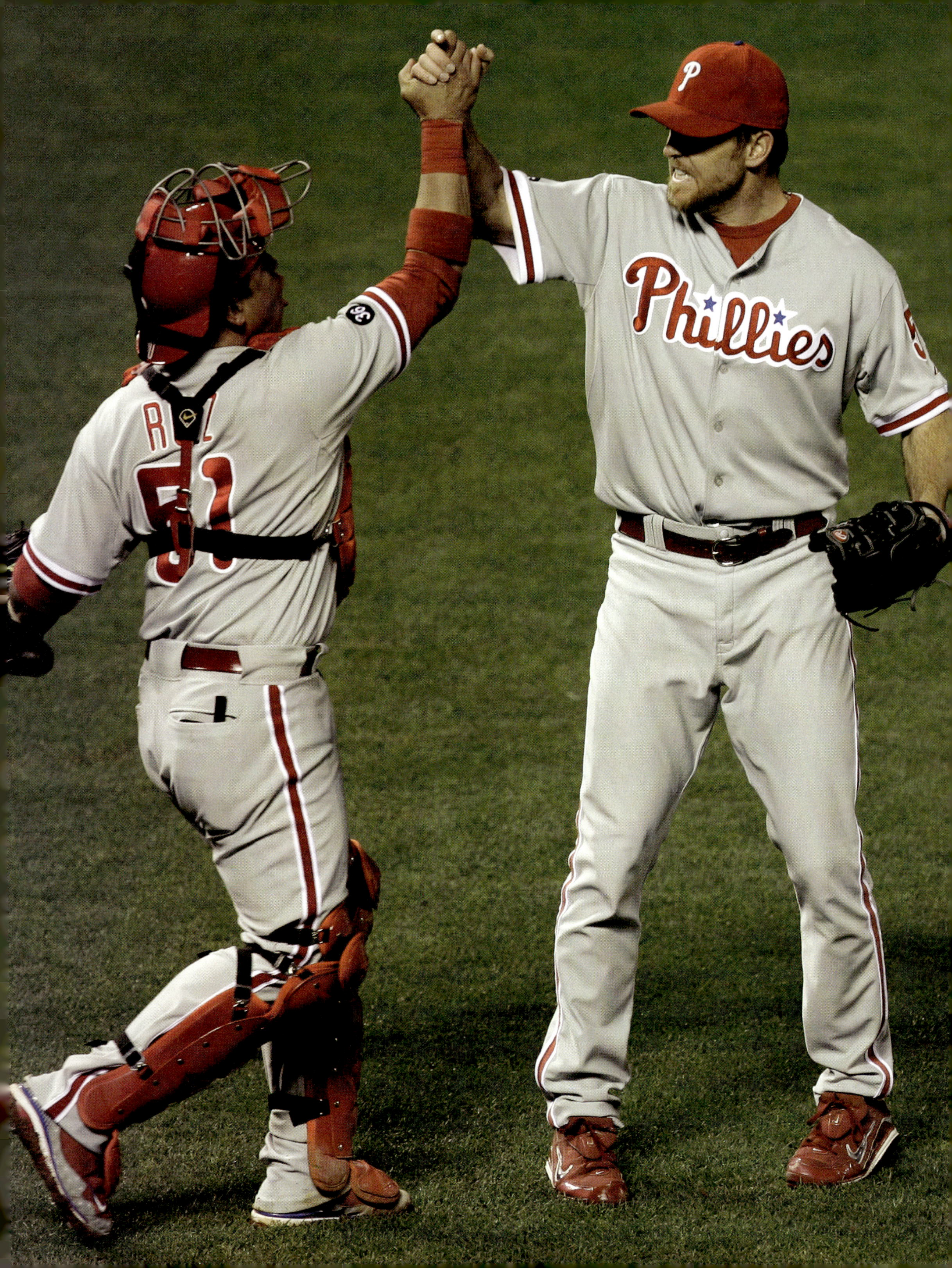
Phillies

3

The Bullpen

While baseball is still the same game that we all grew up with—three strikes per out, three outs per inning, and 27 outs in a nine-inning game—the way that those last outs are approached has changed drastically. There was a time, not all that long ago, when a starting pitcher was expected to finish what he started. It was almost a macho thing that called into question a starting pitcher's toughness if he was unable to pitch deep into ball games.

Big contracts and the worry of injury to top starters led to pitch counts, which limit the number of pitches most starters are allowed to throw in a game. There were times when it was not out of the ordinary to see a starting pitcher throw 150 pitches in a game. Now warning bells and alarms go off as a starter reaches the 100-pitch point.

Gene Garber was an outstanding relief pitcher who spent 19 years in the major leagues pitching for four teams including the Phillies and the Atlanta Braves, with whom he still holds the team saves record. He is no fan of pitch counts and the way the pitchers are used today.

"Pitch counts are the biggest farce in the game," he said. "It only tells a guy when he should be getting tired. If I have thrown 90 pitches, then I must be getting tired. Not true. If you learn to pitch properly and get into a good rhythm, you can throw 200 pitches, which won't tax your arm as much as throwing 40 pitches out of sync. A lot of baseball is run by people who haven't played the game.

"With pitch counts you are telling a guy when he should be getting tired and giving him an excuse to come out of a game."

In earlier times, relief pitchers were the guys who were not good enough to start, older veterans trying to hold on to big-league glory for another season and young pitchers deemed not quite ready to challenge for a spot in the rotation. But over the years with the effectiveness of pitchers such as Johnny Murphy, Joe Page, Hoyt Wilhelm, Jim Konstanty, Elroy Face, and a host of others, relief

The 2011 season is Brad Lidge's fourth as the Phillies' closer after being acquired from Houston after the 2007 season. Lidge saved 27 games for the Phillies in 2010.

pitching has become an honorable profession. But "closers" in those days were known as short relievers and when called upon would pitch anywhere between one and three innings. The specialization of today's game was not part of the equation.

Pitch counts begat more innings out of the bullpen and the increased specialization of the game. Tony La Russa and his Hall of Fame closer Dennis Eckersley changed the role of the reliever as well with the advent of the one-inning close. Most of the strategy of a baseball game now comes from the back of the bullpen forward. Every team has a bevy of relief specialists including the closer, setup man, lefty specialist, long man, and mop-up man. Every pitcher has a specific job and every job has a specific pitcher.

While some teams have tried to buck the trend with a closer by committee, where different pitchers are thrown into that role at different times, the successful teams have a clear road map of each pitcher's responsibility. In that respect, the Phillies are no different.

Moving from the back of the pen forward, Brad Lidge enters his fourth year as the Phillies' closer. It is also the final year of his contract, another variable to keep in mind as the season progresses. Will he get a contract extension, or will the team consider moving someone else into that spot in the future? His setup man has been hard-throwing right-hander Ryan Madson, a role which the angular hurler seems to relish. Jose Contreras returns for his second year as a Phillie after a good season in 2010.

Also returning is left-handed specialist J.C. Romero, who needs to rebound from a pair of inconsistent seasons. Danys Baez had an up-and-down year for the team and young David Herndon, a Rule 5 draftee who had to remain with the big club for the entire season, showed much promise, as has another young lefty, Antonio Bastardo. Chad Durbin will not return after three seasons with the Phillies.

The health of Lidge remains a key element to the success of the bullpen and, of course, the team in general. When healthy, Lidge remains one of the premier closers in the game. And last season, he made a successful switch from a hard thrower who quite regularly tried to blow hitters away into more of a pitcher who used not only his fastball, but an outstanding slider to fool hitters and keep them off balance. If he can stay healthy and continue to pitch in such a matter, there is no reason to believe that he won't improve on his 27 save performance in 2010.

Madson is coming off a year in which he was once again effective (after returning from a stint on the disabled list after his toe lost a battle with a locker room chair). His velocity seems to have increased and he still possesses one of the best change-ups in the game. The veteran, former starter Contreras has made the change from starter to reliever and even contributed four saves last season. He will be counted on to maintain his innings and possibly pick up some of those from the departed Durbin.

J.C. Romero could be a very important cog in the bullpen in 2011, but he needs to regain his effectiveness, which basically means the ability to throw strikes. If he can do that, his value to the team increases tenfold. Danys Baez was very inconsistent in 2010, as he's been for much of his career. But he still throws hard, in the mid-90s. Unfortunately, he still throws straight.

While the team had to keep Herndon last season, his propensity to throw ground balls can make him a valuable member of the bullpen. Last year's big-league experience no doubt will make him a better pitcher. Antonio Bastardo has had very little opportunity to prove himself, but his arm is alive. Another rookie, Vance Worley, looked impressive, and Scott Mathieson, recovering from his second Tommy John surgery, is another option out of the bullpen.

So while much of the Phillies' roster and pitching staff seem set, there are some opportunities. The fifth starter will be either Joe Blanton or Kyle Kendrick. The odd man out could very well be the long man out of the pen. Can Bastardo push Romero for the lefty-specialist job? There will be serious competition between the likes of Baez, Herndon, Worley, and Mathieson. And then there is always the possibility of a young pitcher catching light in a bottle and winning a spot on the roster in spring training.

So while the defending National League East champions seem to have a very set roster and pitching staff, opportunity awaits for a returning vet or a younger pitcher to earn a spot in the bullpen.

It should be an interesting spring training. ■

Other than sustaining a broken right toe after kicking a chair in the Phillies' clubhouse following a blown save in April, Ryan Madson had another fine season for the Phillies in 2010. The right-hander posted a 6–2 record and a 2.55 ERA in 55 appearances.

BRAD LIDGE 54

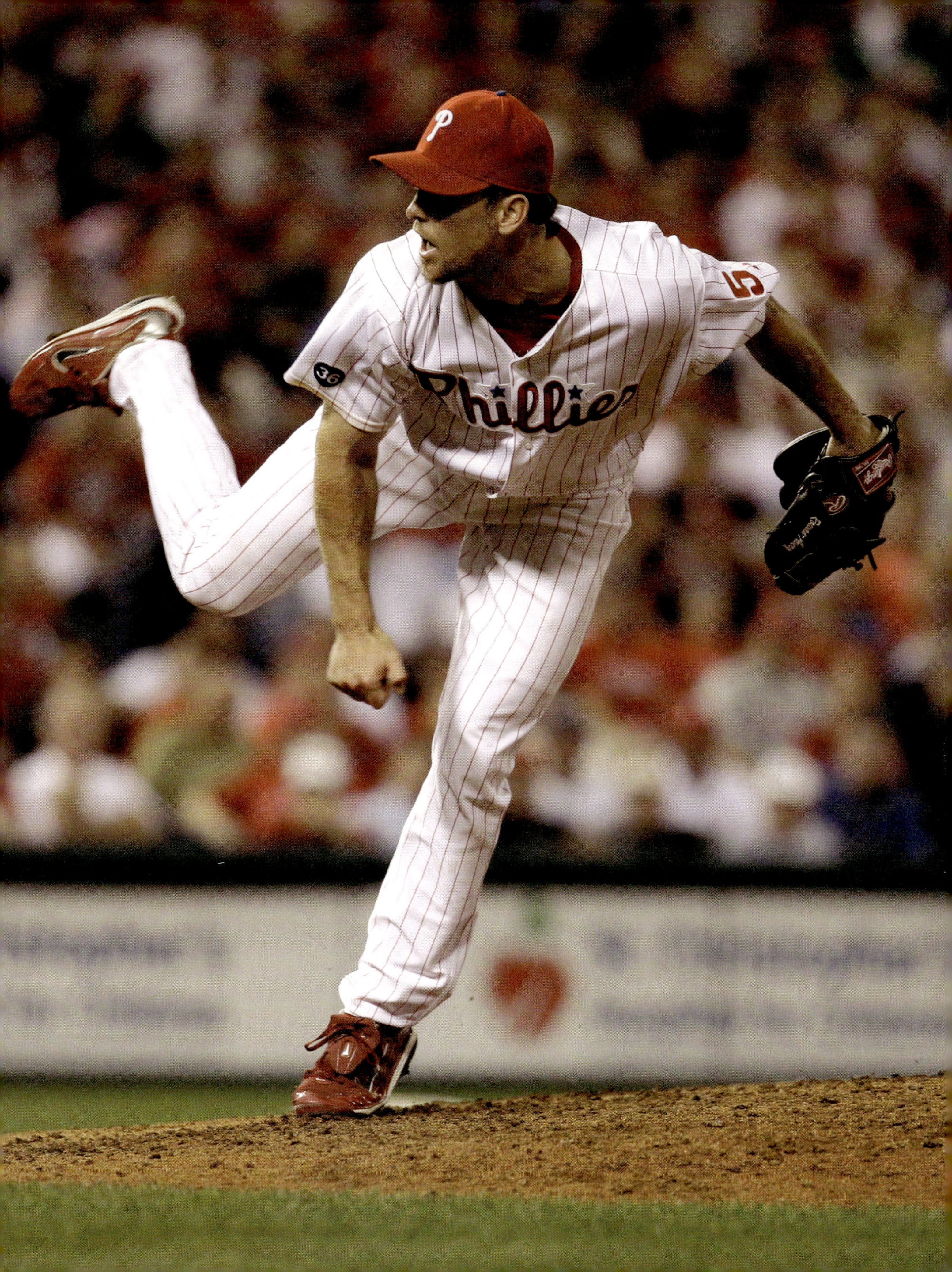
Phillies

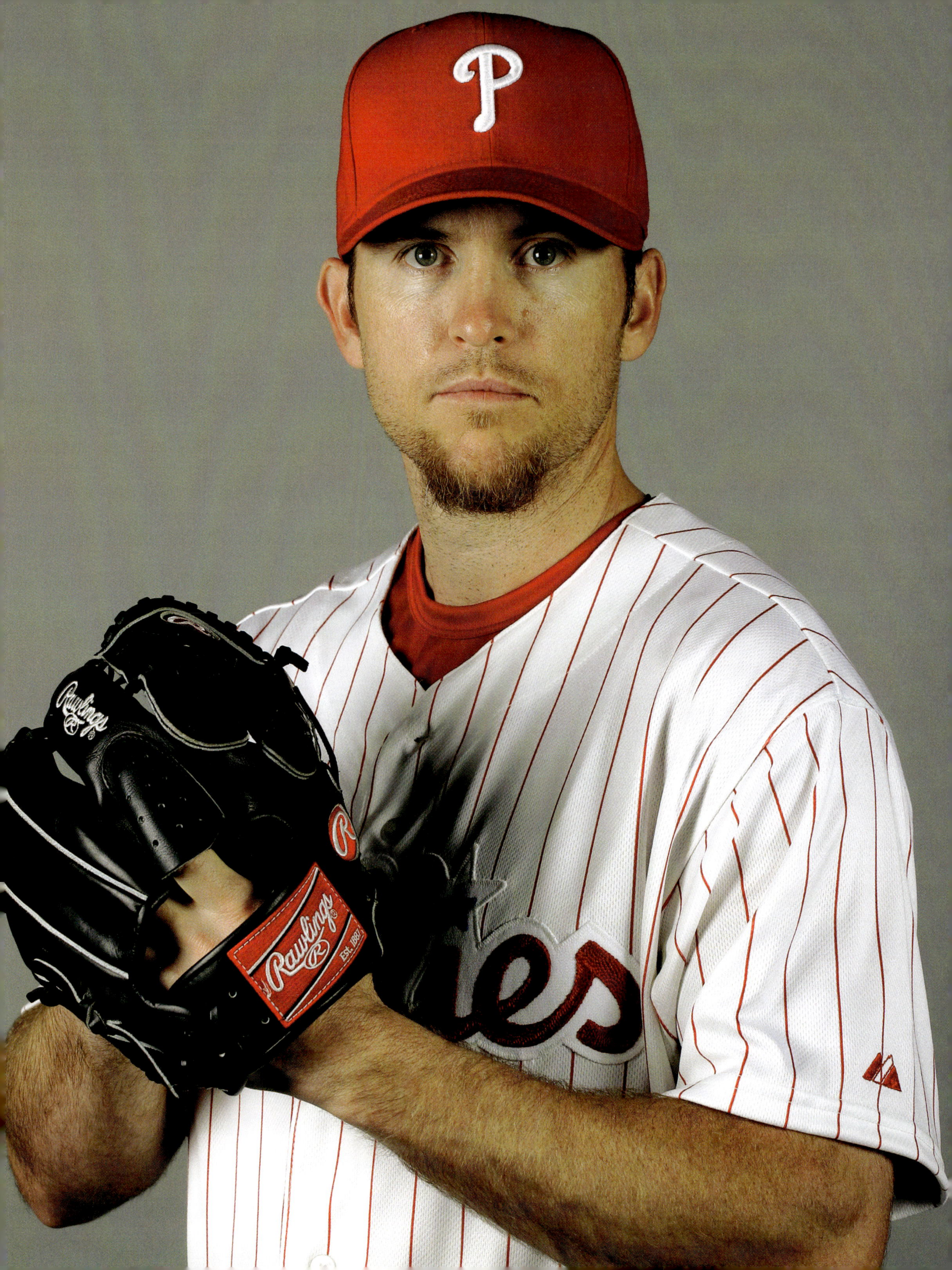
Rawlings
Rawlings

54
Brad Lidge

Born: December 23, 1976 | Ht: 6'5" | Wt: 210 lbs | B: R | T: R

	W-L	ERA	Games	IP	Hits	S	BB	K
2010:	1-1	2.96	50	45.2	32	27	24	52
Career:	26-29	3.51	567	574.2	464	222	263	766

A generation before, in 1980, the image of closer Tug McGraw striking out Willie Wilson of the Kansas City Royals to end the World Series and bring the World Championship to Philadelphia was permanently etched in the minds, hearts, and souls of Phillies fans. A similar experience was felt by those who watched Brad Lidge fan Eric Hinske to end the 2008 Fall Classic and bring Philadelphia its second baseball Championship. For those who witnessed both, pure baseball heaven on Earth.

Lidge was one of baseball's finest closers when he was acquired by the Phillies in November 2007 along with infielder Eric Bruntlett, in exchange for pitcher Geoff Geary, outfielder Michael Bourn, and infield prospect Mike Costanzo. That move determined that Brett Myers, converted to a closer the previous season, would return to the starting rotation for the 2008 campaign.

In five years closing games for Houston, Lidge had accumulated 123 saves including 29 in 2004, 42 in 2005, and 32 in 2006. But the following season he was demoted from the closer's role for a time and while he did save 19 games, he blew eight other save opportunities. Feeling that he might be in need of a change of scenery, the Phillies jumped on the chance to bring Lidge to Philadelphia.

He arrived to spring training in 2008 with a surgically-repaired knee that would require more minor surgery prior to the start of the regular season. Coming off a subpar season with an injured knee, Lidge also arrived in Philadelphia with that "Lights Out" mentality that made him such a good closer.

But no one in their wildest dreams could imagine what Brad Lidge had in store for the Phillies in 2008. He was perfect. Literally. With a 2–0 record and a 1.96 ERA in 72 games, he silenced his Houston critics and thrilled his Philadelphia supporters by converting 41 consecutive save opportunities during the regular sea-

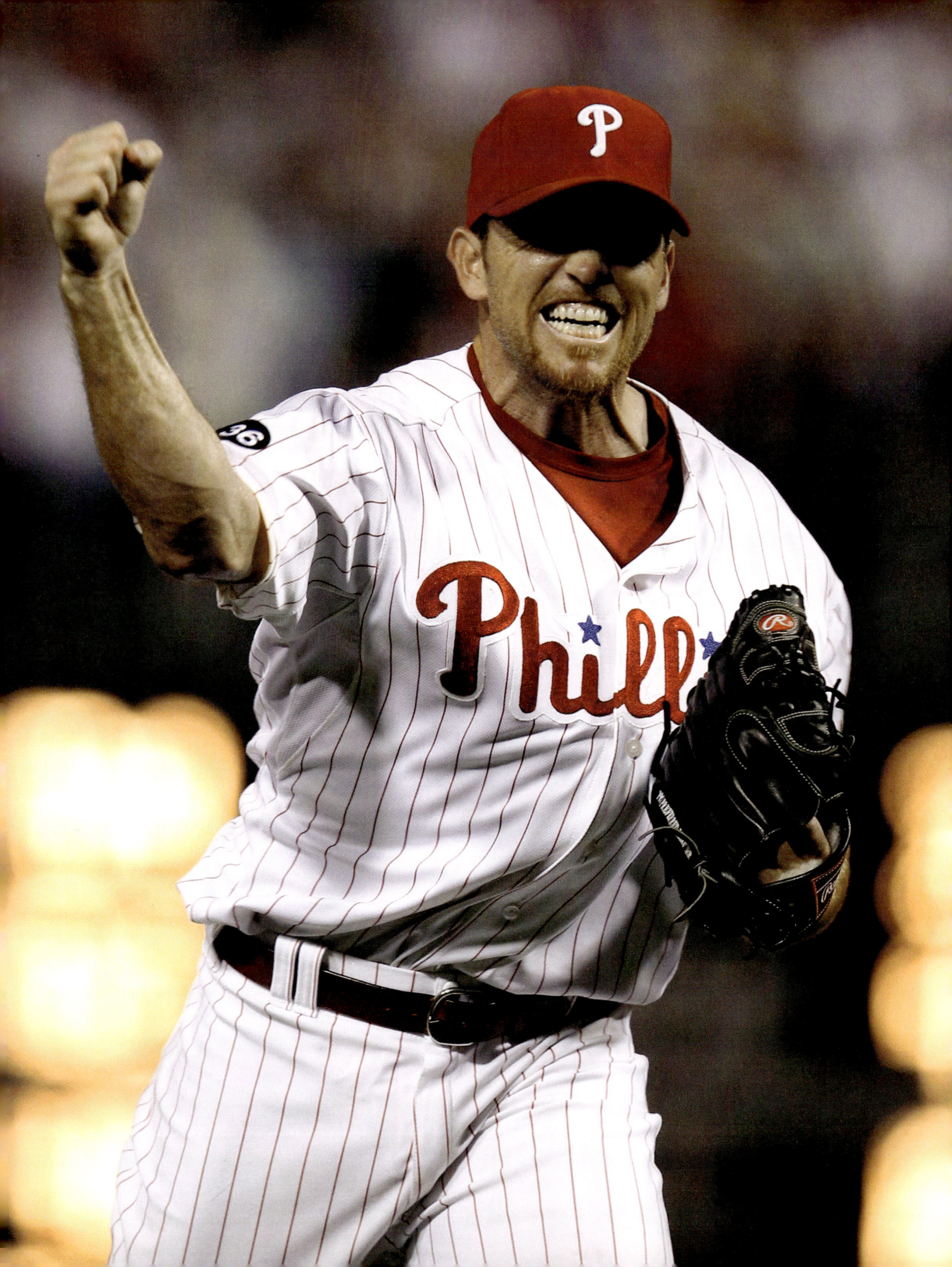
P
36
Phill

son, and adding seven more in the postseason. He was perfect. Forty-eight save opportunities and he converted every single one of them. Of course, that kind of a performance sets the bar pretty high. Once you're perfect, anything less stands out like a sore thumb.

"Brad is a very intelligent person," said Jamie Moyer. "He wants nothing but success. In '08 he was perfect. It's really hard to repeat something like that. In the city of Philadelphia, when you show you are able there is an expectation. He had a couple surgeries with the elbow and the knee and hopefully that is all behind him now.

"He wants to be the closer. On days that he is not effective I know it eats at him. But he comes back ready the next day."

Whether it was a sore thumb, bad knee, cranky elbow, or just the baseball gods keeping him on his toes, Brad Lidge was nowhere near the same pitcher in 2009, as his 0–8 record and 7.21 ERA will attest. He got off to a bad start, which was only made worse by a stint on the disabled list in June with an injured knee. When he returned in late June things didn't go much better. At various points of the second half of the season he was used in non-save situations, and although he blew 11 save opportunities he converted 31 others.

Through good times and bad, the closer has to be able to stay centered and not get too high or too low. Brad Lidge seems to have that kind of personality.

"He's a pro," said Chris Wheeler, "a non-complainer who doesn't make excuses. Even when the bad stuff was going on he never gave up on himself. He is the type of guy who can handle the closing role. The job can make you crazy because it is one of the hardest jobs on the team. They go out there after a starter has done a great job and can blow it and have to live with it. They have a different mindset and different stomachs. I'm a big Brad Lidge guy. You can always talk to him and he's a pleasant guy. When he's healthy, just turn him loose."

After getting his elbow surgically repaired in January 2010, Brad Lidge was healthy. He responded with a 1–1 record in 50 games with a 2.96 ERA with 27 saves and just five blown saves. Sometimes it was a high-wire act, but much more often than not he got the job done.

He was much closer to 2008 last year than he was in 2009. He was healthier and he also altered his pitching strategy.

"In the past he threw a lot of sliders," said Jamie Moyer. "Last year I think at times teams were laying off his slider so he had to use his fastball more and be more effective with it. That is one of the hurdles he was working on. You've got so many things going on that you are tinkering with to get better and for Brad that was the key."

Also, not that Lidge needs any added motivation, but he enters 2011 in the last year of his contract. He would like to stay with the Phillies and was instrumental in convincing his former Houston teammate, Roy Oswalt, to accept a trade to the team. A healthy, motivated Lidge coming off a good season could mean an even better year in 2011. ∎

Brad Lidge followed a record-setting 2008 season with a disappointing and injury-riddled 2009 campaign, but bounced back to save 27 games for the Phillies in 2010.

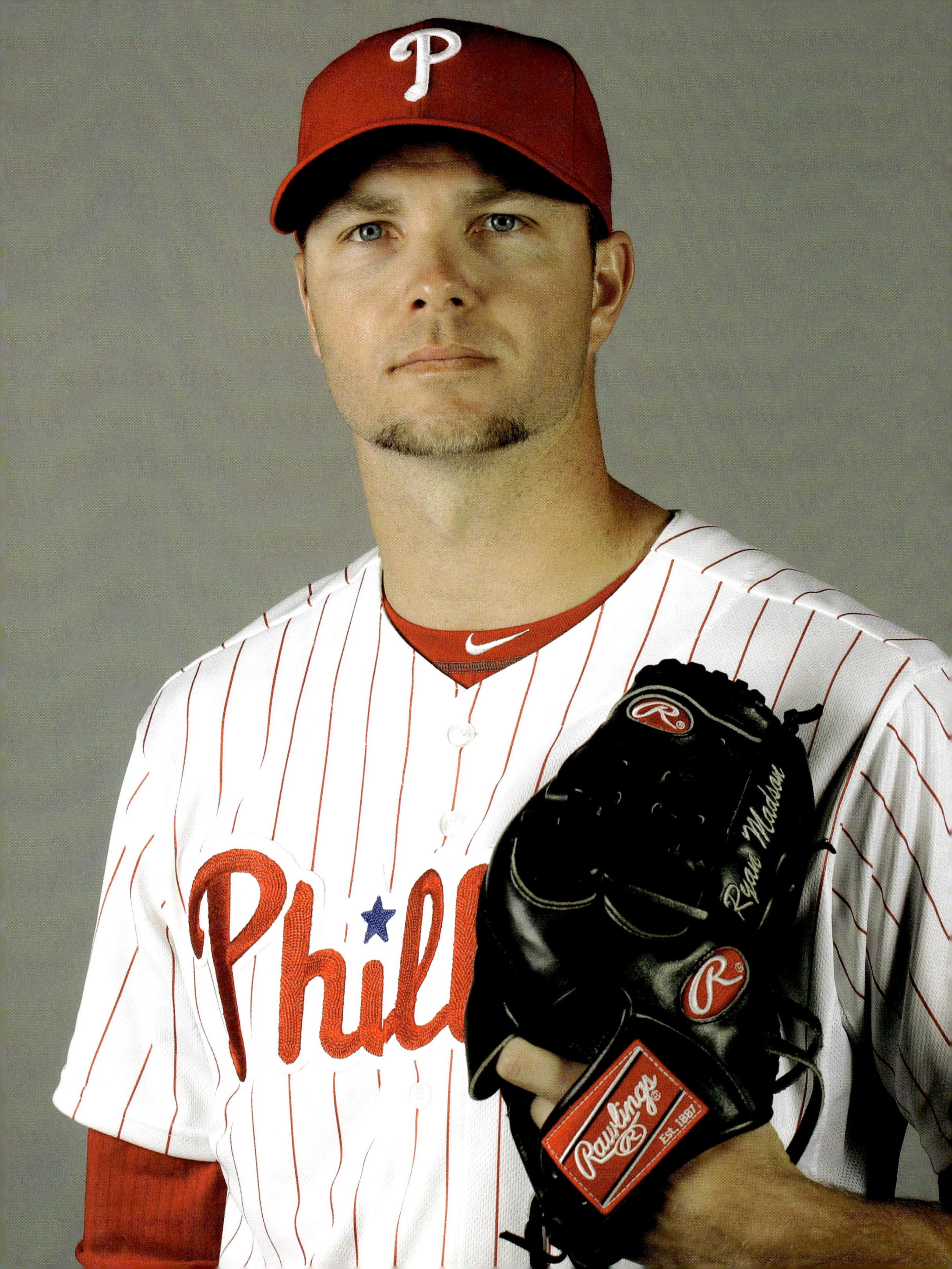
Phil
Ryan Madson
Rawlings
Est. 1887

46
Ryan Madson

	W–L	ERA	Games	IP	Hits	S	BB	K
**Born: August 28, 1980	Ht: 6'6"	Wt: 195 lbs	B: L	T: R**					
2010:	6–2	2.55	55	53	42	5	13	64
Career:	43–28	3.71	429	569.1	570	20	175	485

Ryan "Mad Dog" Madson had his chance to start some games for the Phillies in 2006. The experiment had mixed results. But since that time he has excelled in baseball's newest specialty role — the setup man.

Madson's job, more often than not, is to come into the game, usually when the Phillies are tied or have the lead, and hold. He is "The Bridge to Lidge." By the time the eighth inning rolls around it's time for Madson to hold the game in check and get it to the ninth inning and closer Brad Lidge. Using a fastball often clocked in the high-90s, a cutter, and a nearly unhittable circle-change, Mad Dog has been a dependable pitcher for Charlie Manuel in his setup role.

Madson had a fine year in 2010 as his 6–2 record and 2.55 ERA indicate. And even though he pitched in 55 games, he missed time on the disabled list as a result of toe surgery necessitated by his losing a war with a clubhouse chair after a troublesome outing. But he rebounded nicely and played a vital part in the Phillies' fourth consecutive division title.

While his season ended in extreme disappointment as he served up the eighth inning home run by San Francisco's Juan Uribe that propelled the Giants into the World Series, Madson showed the maturity and mindset of a successful reliever after the game.

"It was shocking for me," he said. "I know the pitch wasn't terrible. He hit it good. I have to give him credit. He hit it good enough to just get it in the front row there. You are always taught that if they beat you that way, you tip your hat. And he beat me. Obviously, he's a great hitter."

Just as obvious, with his ability and demeanor, Ryan Madson could someday follow the likes of Mariano Rivera and Francisco Rodriguez, who both went from successful setup men to very successful closers. ■

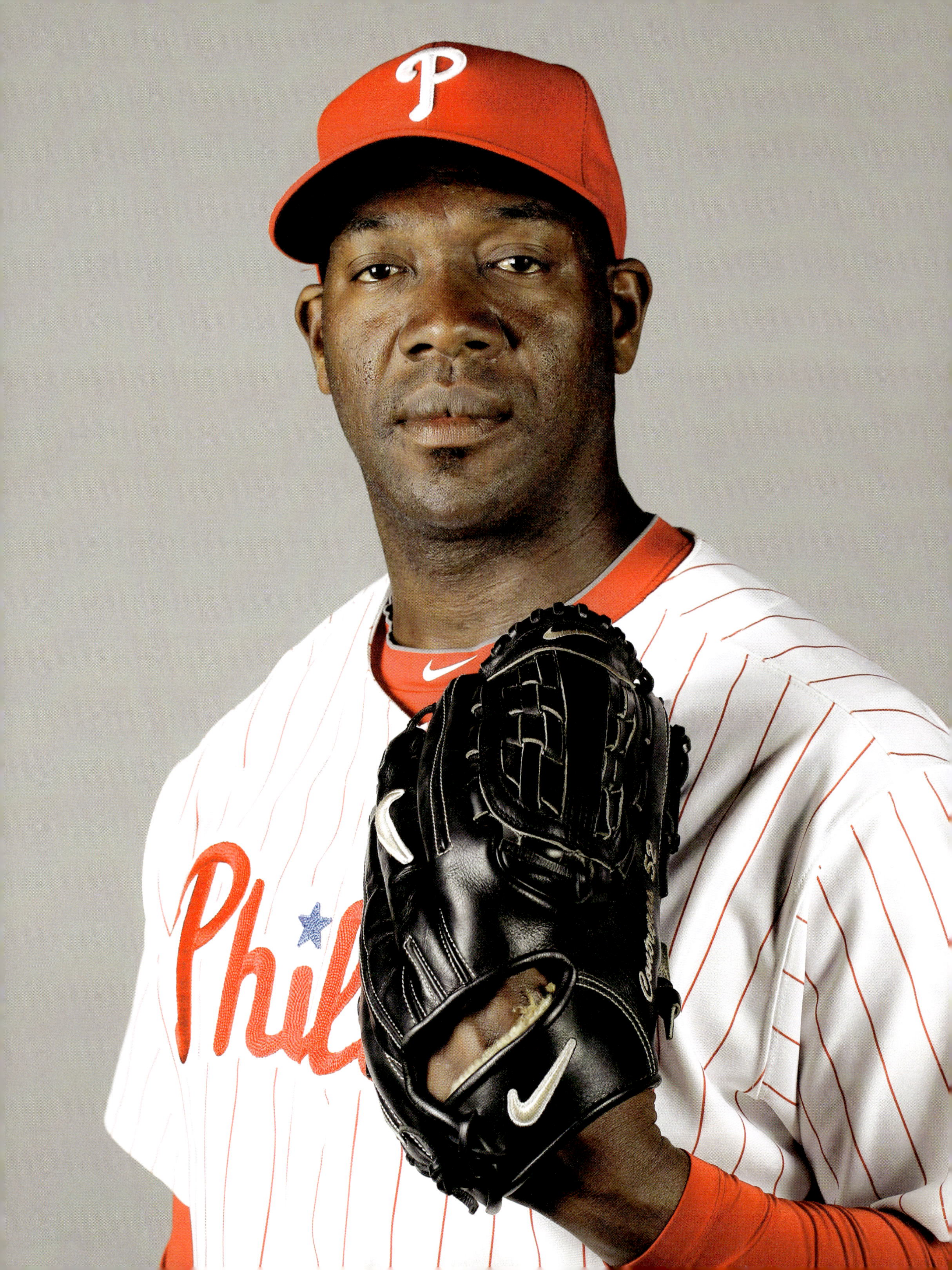
Phil

52
Jose Contreras

Born: December 6, 1971 | Ht: 6'4" | Wt: 245 lbs | B: R | T: R

	W-L	ERA	Games	IP	Hits	S	BB	K
2010:	6-4	3.34	67	56.2	53	4	16	57
Career:	77-67	4.55	258	1140.1	1145	4	410	856

This big, hard-throwing right-hander was very much an unknown quantity when he was signed by the Phillies prior to the 2010 season. A seven-year veteran, Contreras had seen good times and bad since defecting from Cuba in October 2002. But he fit right in to the Phillies' bullpen, where he was used exclusively as a reliever for the first time in his career.

Used in different roles by skipper Charlie Manuel, Contreras also earned the first four saves of his career, filling in for an injured Brad Lidge. His electric stuff was as good as ever, resulting in many uncomfortable at-bats for opposing hitters. His trek to Philadelphia is one of the more interesting ones.

Contreras was the Cuban Athlete of the Year on three different occasions. But the desire to pitch in the major leagues led to his defection. Signed by the New York Yankees, he went 7–2 in 2003. The following July he was dealt to the Chicago White Sox. He finished that season with a 13–9 mark between the two clubs but soon became a regular with the ChiSox, going 15–7 in 2005 (including a 3–1 mark in the post-season on the way to a World Series victory) and 13–9 in 2006 before slumping to 10–17 the following year.

In 2008 he continued to take the ball every turn with varying results. He was 7–6 early in August when he ruptured his Achilles tendon fielding a ground ball, forcing him to miss the remainder of the season.

Things got worse in 2009 as Contreras wound up being 5–13 with Chicago, endured a stint in the minor leagues, and was finally traded to Colorado. With the Rockies he was very effective in seven appearances out of the bullpen, which piqued the Phillies' interest in having him fill that role in Philadelphia.

His successful 2010 season has the organization feeling confident in his ability to once again be a powerful force out of the bullpen in 2011.

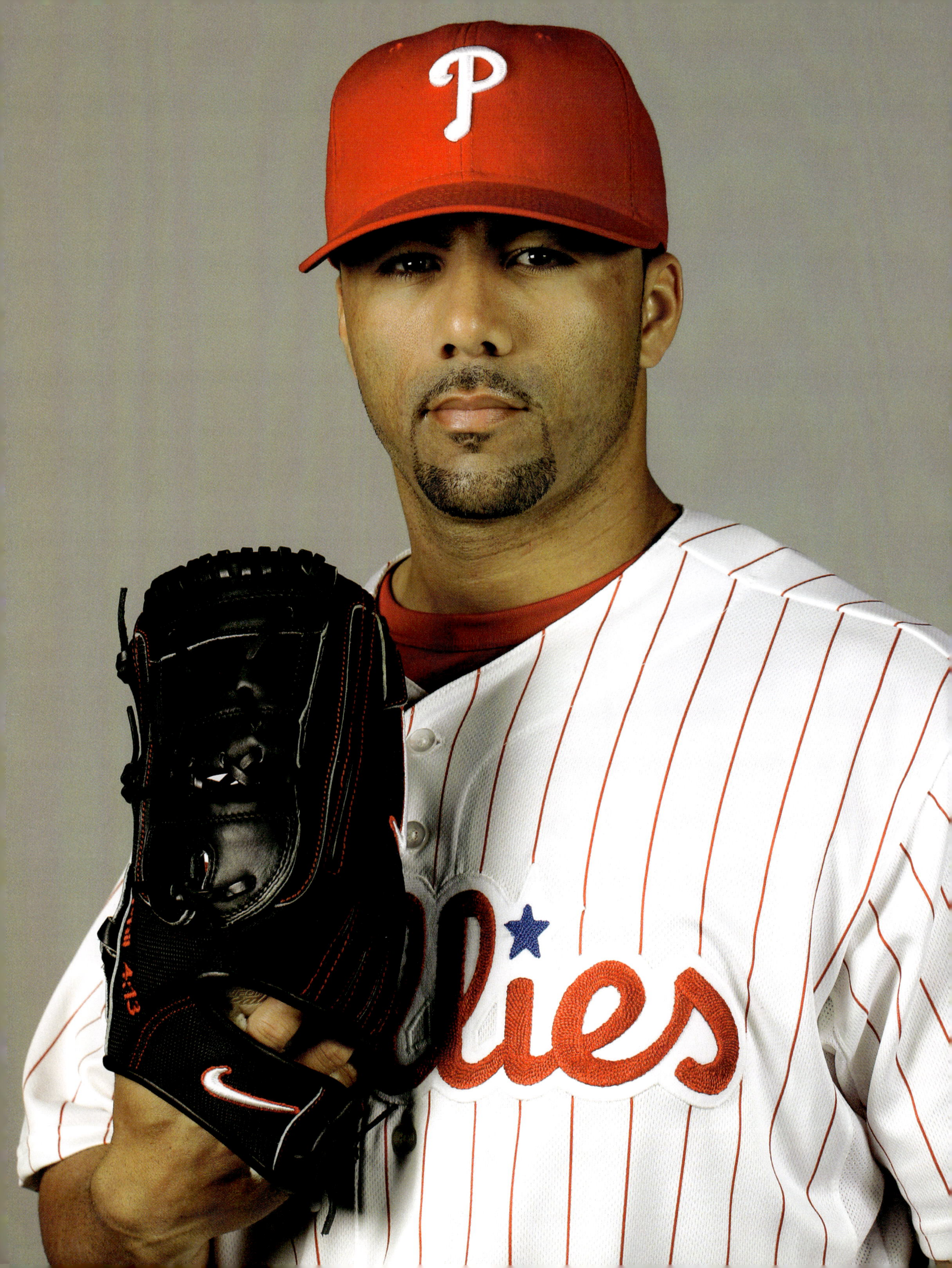

16
J.C. Romero

Born: June 4, 1976 | Ht: 5'11" | Wt: 205 lbs | B: B | T: L

	W–L	ERA	Games	IP	Hits	S	BB	K
2010:	1–0	3.68	60	36.2	30	3	29	28
Career:	33–28	4.08	628	624.2	575	7	357	501

A good description of J.C. Romero has often been a good description of many big-league pitchers. He is as effective as his control is good. But that being said, he's good enough to be entering his 13th season in the bigs.

While it was a pretty good bet that the talented lefty would be coming out of some big-league bullpen in 2011, there was certainly no guarantee that he would be returning to Philadelphia for his fifth season as his contract was not picked up by the Phillies, who had an option to retain him. Later in the off-season though, they agreed on a one-year contract to bring him back.

Romero was actually a starting pitcher early in his career while pitching for the Minnesota Twins in 2000 and 2001. But his 3–11 combined record over those two seasons resulted in new responsibilities in the Twins bullpen, where he prospered. In 2002, he went 9–2 with a 1.89 ERA in 81 games.

Following the 2005 season, Romero became a man on the move. He was dealt to the Los Angeles Angels, where he pitched for one year, appearing in 65 games. But his 1–2 record and 6.70 ERA turned him into a free agent after the season. He signed with the Boston Red Sox where he was 1–0 with a 3.15 ERA in 2007. But his wildness caused his release by the BoSox, and he was then signed by the Phillies.

Romero finished out the 2007 season strong in Philadelphia, going 1–2 with a 1.25 ERA in 51 games. He still wild, but talented enough to get out of jams.

His best season may well have been 2008. Romero appeared in 81 games with a 4–4 record and a 2.75 ERA. He was stellar in the postseason, not allowing a run in seven innings to help the Phillies win the World Series. And he became the first native of Puerto Rico to win two games in the Fall Classic.

Both he and the Phillies hope for his return to 2008 form and a Philadelphia championship in 2011. ∎

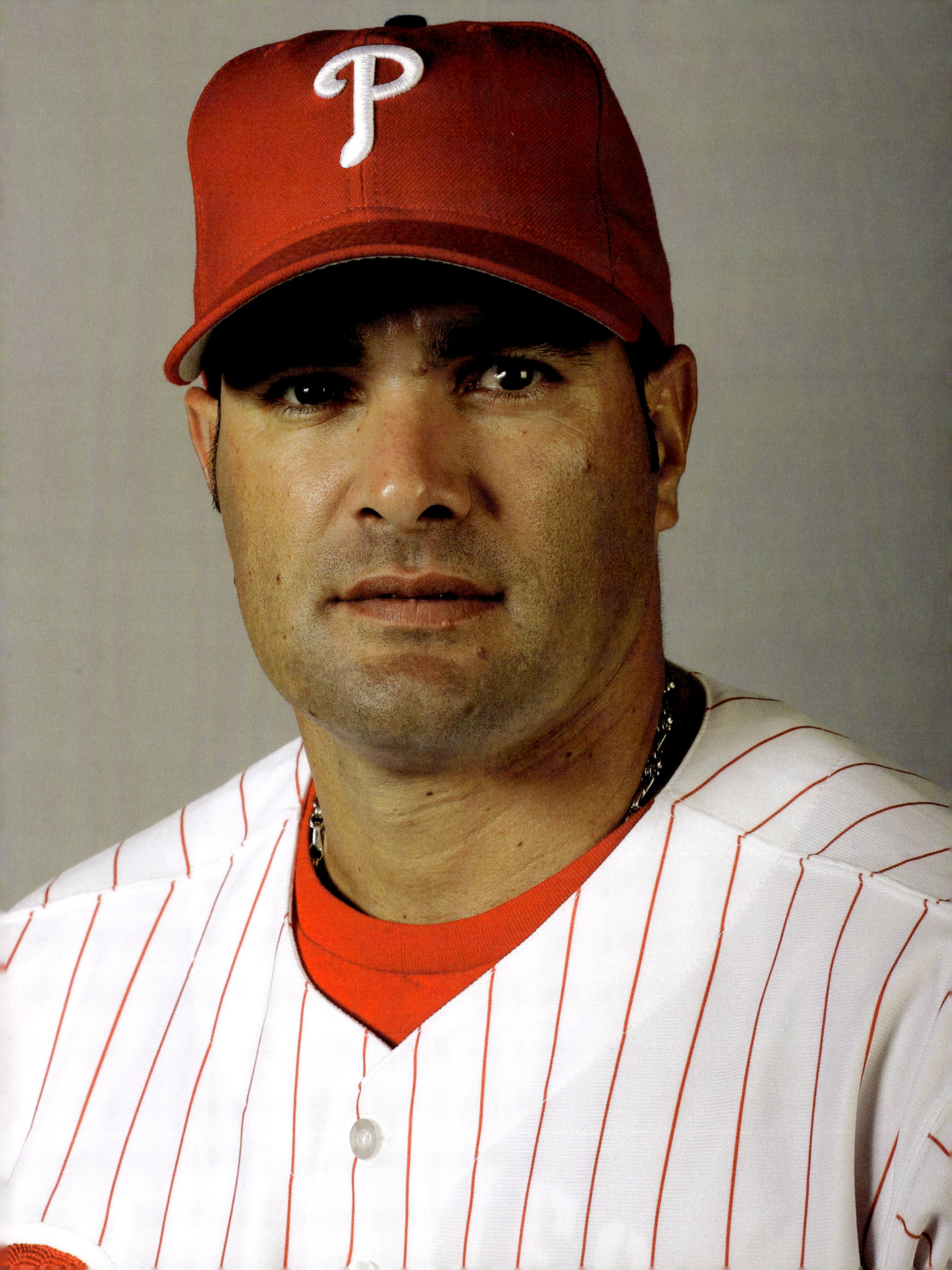

55
Danys Baez

Born: September 10, 1977 | Ht: 6'3" | Wt: 235 lbs | B: R | T: R

	W–L	ERA	Games	IP	Hits	S	BB	K
2010:	3–4	5.48	51	47.2	55	0	23	28
Career:	38–53	4.14	504	661	609	114	275	487

It was a nice homecoming for Danys Baez when he joined his friend and fellow Cuban Jose Contreras in the Phillies' bullpen. While Contreras thrived in his new role, Baez pitched well at times but had a very inconsistent season. He seems completely recovered from the 2008 arm surgery that caused him to miss that entire season, and he still throws hard, bringing his heater to the plate in the mid-90s. But he also seems to throw the ball straight much of the time, giving big-league hitters ample opportunity to succeed.

Baez broke into The Show in 2001 with Cleveland, going 5–3. He was a starter for the Tribe for most of the following season with a 10–11 record and a 4.41 ERA. Made the closer in August of that year, Baez contributed six saves. But the following year he had a 2–9 record in 73 games and a 3.81 ERA. While he contributed 25 saves, he led the league with 10 blown saves. Not offered a contract for the following season, he got a three-year deal with Tampa Bay.

He pitched well in his first two years in Tampa Bay, accumulating a combined 9–8 record with 71 saves. But things started to fall apart in 2006, following a trade to the Los Angeles Dodgers where he lost his closer's job after blowing his first four save opportunities. Another deal saw him land in Atlanta with the Braves.

Making the switch from closer to setup man had helped Baez, who signed a three-year deal with the Baltimore Orioles. But he was 0–6 the first year, missed all of 2008, and was 4–6 in 2009.

That inconsistency followed him to Philadelphia, where he will be in a battle for his spot on the Phillies' roster in 2011. ∎

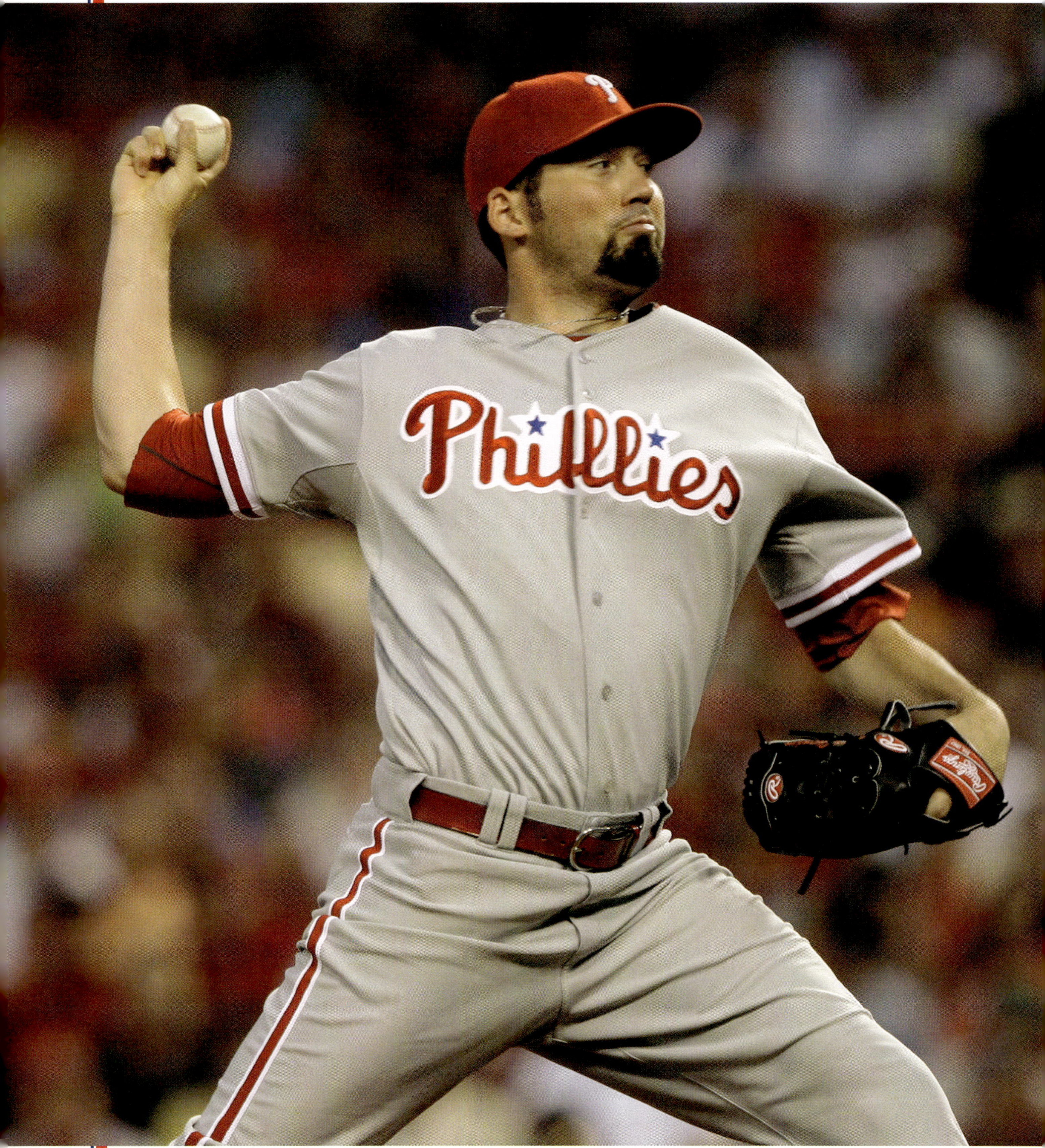
Phillies

57 | 58 | 49
David Herndon | Antonio Bastardo | Vance Worley

Every year, young pitchers make a mark on a pitching staff. Whether it's a Rule 5 draftee who must remain with the big club all season long, a young pitcher still trying to find his spot on the team, or a prospect getting his first big-league look, competition on a pitching staff never ends.

All three of these young pitchers, Herndon, Bastardo, and Worley, fill one of those parameters. Herndon was a highly thought of Rule 5 pick from a year ago who pitched his way onto the big club in spring training. Bastardo is a home-grown Phillies product who could very well challenge J.C. Romero for the left-handed specialist position on the roster. And Vance Worley pitched well after his late-season call up.

Herndon, 24, was taken from the Anaheim Angels organization and appeared in 47 games for the Phillies with a 1–3 record and a 4.30 ERA. With great downward movement on his pitches, he is a ground ball pitcher. At some times those ground balls seem to have eyes going through the infield, but he also has the kind of stuff to get out of troublesome innings with ground ball double plays.

Bastardo, 25, was signed by the Phillies organization in 2005 and has made a name for himself showing flashes of a good major league pitcher. He is a combined 4–3 in 31 games during 2009 and 2010 and is unscored upon in three postseason games. His biggest moment was in the National League Division Series in 2009 against Colorado when he struck out Jason Giambi with two outs and the bases loaded. He remains the biggest challenge to J.C. Romero's spot in the bullpen.

Worley, 23, was drafted in the third round of the Amateur Draft in 2008. His rapid ascent through the Phillies' farm system culminated in two stints with the big club in 2010. Not showing any sign of nerves or concern, the young right-hander went 1–1 with a 1.38 ERA in five games. His demeanor and command on the pitching mound drew rave reviews from all who saw him. In those five games, he pitched 13 innings, yielding just eight hits and two runs. But he also had good control, walking four while fanning 12. And unlike Herndon and Bastardo, Worley could also be considered one of the alternatives for that fifth starting spot depending on what the organization does with Joe Blanton and Kyle Kendrick.

So while the Phillies' pitching staff seems very much set for four-fifths of the starting rotation, there is still much to be decided in the bullpen. In that respect it should be a very interesting spring training in Clearwater, Florida. ■

David Herndon appeared in 47 games for the Phillies in 2010.

Armed & Dangerous

4

The Starting Eight—Plus

The Phillies' pitching staff gave what was expected of them in 2010. It seems very often like pitching is the key element of any team's chances for success. Remember, good pitching usually stops good hitting. And the Phillies' staff did more than their part. But a lineup with the likes of Ryan Howard, Chase Utley, Jimmy Rollins, Shane Victorino, and Raul Ibanez would be expected to make a mark. However, a look back at the offensive production of this team of talented stars showed that in 2010, Philadelphia was the seventh best offensive team in baseball.

Their 772 runs were behind the New York Yankees, Boston Red Sox, Tampa Bay Rays, Cincinnati Reds, Texas Rangers, and Minnesota Twins. It's not that they were bad. The Phillies trot out as dangerous a lineup as there is in Major League Baseball. Their lineup includes two former National League Most Valuable Players in Howard and Rollins as well as someone who is considered by many to be the best player in the league not to win an MVP award in Utley. But in spite of the talented and powerful starting eight, there were countless times during the regular season and the playoffs when the offense was not the game-changing element that it had been in the past.

Certainly, injuries played a part. Rollins played in a career-low 88 games and hit a very pedestrian .243. Utley missed time as well, playing in 115 games and hitting .275. And even Ryan Howard fought through a painful foot injury that changed his batting stride and limited him to 31 home runs and 108 RBIs.

So the team goes into the 2011 season with these question marks. Could the injuries be just an expected part of the game that goes in cycles and affects teams at various times, or could the problems of 2010 be the beginning of a pattern? After all, the offensive nucleus of the team is all over 30 years of age. Is father time

Phillies manager Charlie Manuel fields a 2008 lineup featuring several popular players familiar to Phillies fans.

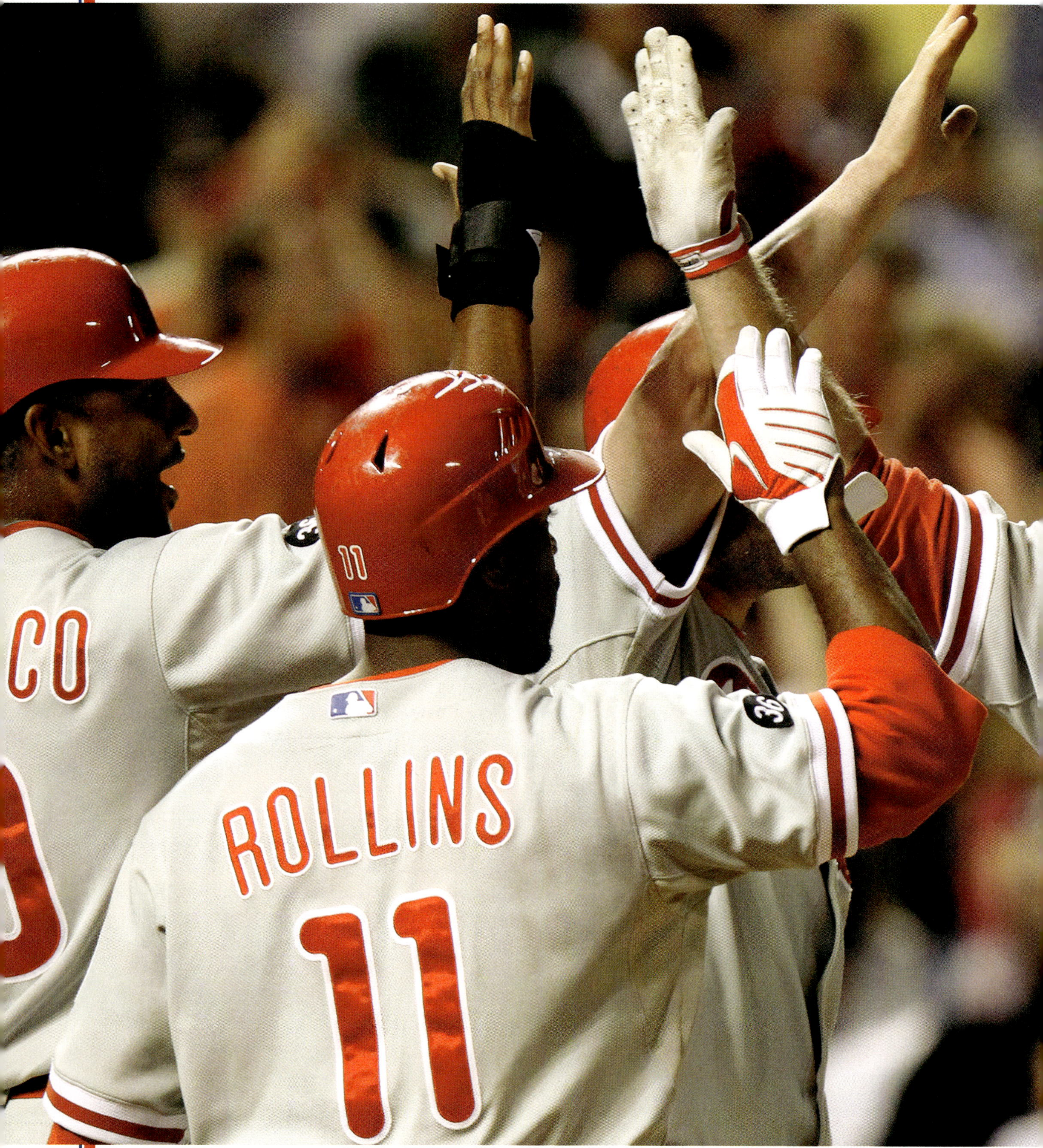
ROLLINS
11

rearing his ugly head, or was it just a year when some key players were hit with physical problems?

"Everybody has concerns about some of the guys getting a little older," said Chris Wheeler. "You wonder if it was an off year where they were getting hurt, or are they going the other way as players? That'll be answered this year. They certainly have a lot of ability. Are they going to put up career numbers? The fact remains that this team is much better on paper than most other teams. But if you see things continue to slide, then you have an idea. I think that it was physical more than anything else last year. But baseball is one of those games where if you have two in a row, it's a pattern."

Add into the mix the departure of right fielder Jayson Werth to the Washington Nationals via free agency. The big slugger had some difficulties in 2010 with runners in scoring position, but the team will still miss his .296 batting average, 27 home runs, 85 RBIs, and 13 stolen bases. He was also an excellent defensive player.

Unless an unexpected trade occurs, the most logical solution seems to be a platoon of sorts between Ben Francisco and Domonic Brown. Of course, Brown could still be sent to Triple A for more seasoning, giving Francisco a shot at the job full time. After all, Werth was a role player until taking over the spot full-time in 2008.

There's talent galore in the Phillies' position players. But there are a number of serious questions that need to be answered. And those answers could go a long way in determining the ultimate success of the 2011 team. Will they win another National League East title? Will they get through the playoffs and once again earn another World Series berth?

Only the regular season will tell. ∎

Second baseman Chase Utley, a five-time All-Star, celebrates after hitting a grand slam against Colorado in 2010.

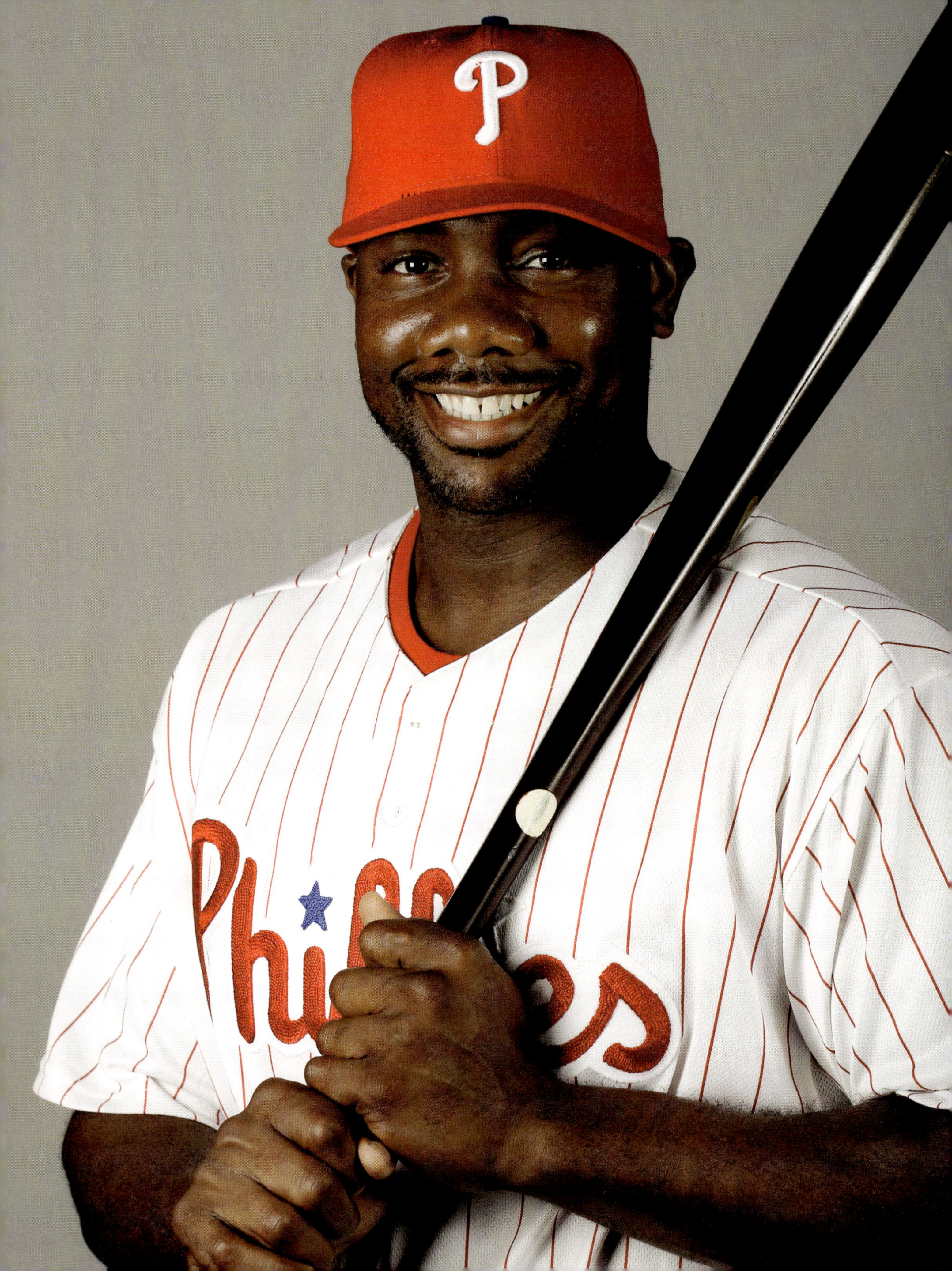

6
Ryan Howard — First Base

Born: November 19, 1979 | Ht: 6′4″ | Wt: 255 lbs | B: L | T: L

	Games	Ave.	Hits	HR	RBI	SB
2010:	143	.276	152	31	108	1
Career:	875	.279	902	253	748	11

Ryan Howard is one of the most recognizable players in Major League Baseball. He is a big, tall, powerful man who uses an extremely open batting stance and holds the bat back, ready to unleash his patented swing. As a result of his propensity to pull the baseball to the right side of the diamond, opposing teams usually employ a severe defensive shift, where the only player near second base is the third baseman.

But in spite of this annoying obstacle, which sees him lose countless hits during the course of a season, Howard remains one of the best players in the game and a true home run threat on every pitch he sees.

His numbers for the 2010 season would be career numbers for just about any other player: 31 homers and 108 runs batted in. But a nagging foot injury hampered the slugging first sacker for much of the last couple of months of the season, which affected his stride. As unfair as it seems, his season was looked at by some as a "down" year. His average production from 2006 through 2009 was 49 homers and 143 RBIs per season. He led the league in home runs in 2006 (58) and 2008 (48) and in RBIs on three different occasions, 2006 (149), 2008 (146), and 2009 (141). He has also drastically improved his defense around the first-base bag.

"The people who think it was an off year for Ryan I think are people who don't really know the game," Jamie Moyer said. "He is a human being who made a major contribution to our team. If you ask any player man-to-man, a teammate making a contribution to your team is the most important thing. When I first came to Philly, Ryan's defense was a little suspect. But Sammy Perlazzo has done a great job of working with him. But it's also really important to understand that Ryan had the ability to understand that he needed to get better. He dropped some weight and his agility got better around the bag. And he's a big man who is a key

Armed & Dangerous

part of that infield who saves a lot of bad throws.

"He plays every day. He's out there 150 or 155 times a year. If guys are not swinging the bat well ahead of him or behind him in the lineup, teams may pitch around him. You see any No. 4 hitter who is getting pitched around and they may go up there and not be as selective as they'd like, just trying to make something happen. So you're hitting with a lot of bad counts. Hitting is not easy and Ryan is a great player and teammate."

Drafted in the fifth round of the 2001 amateur draft, Howard powered his way through the Phillies' farm system before supplanting popular slugger Jim Thome at first base after his elbow injury gave Howard a chance to show off his skills in 2005. In limited action that year he hit .288 with 22 home runs and 63 RBIs, good enough to be named the National League Rookie of the Year.

That off-season the Phillies dealt Thome to the Chicago White Sox and the rest has been history as Howard has continually put up impressive numbers and has also won a Most Valuable Player Award. If he is healthy in 2011, there is little doubt that the slugging Howard will return to form with another monster year. ■

Ryan Howard celebrates after hitting a walk-off home run to beat the Cincinnati Reds in 2010. The 2005 National League Rookie of the Year and 2006 MVP hit 31 home runs for the Phillies in 2010.

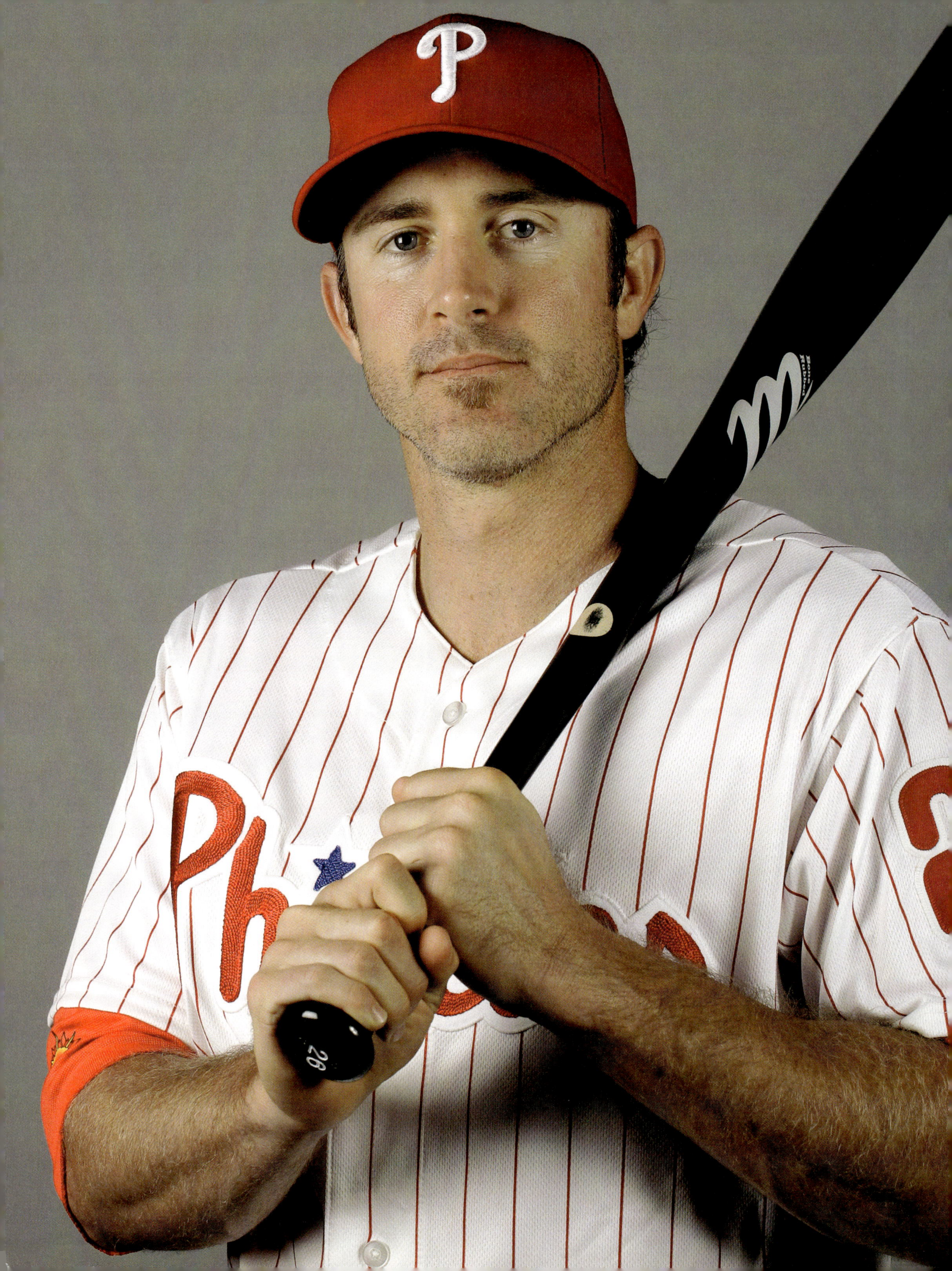
26

26
Chase Utley—Second Base

Born: December 17, 1978 | Ht: 6'1" | Wt: 190 lbs | B: L | T: R

	Games	Ave.	Hits	HR	RBI	SB
2010:	115	.275	117	16	65	13
Career:	1006	.293	1095	177	650	96

Here is a great trivia question for Philadelphia Phillies fans. What do Chase Utley and former Phillie Oscar Gamble have in common? The answer is below.

Another trivia question might identify Chase Utley as the best player not to win a Most Valuable Player Award. A true leader on the team, Utley made quite an impression in his first major league at-bat, smacking a grand-slam home run in front of the home fans in 2003. The first round pick of the 2000 Amateur Draft, Utley split time between Triple A Scranton/Wilkes-Barre and the Phillies in 2003 and 2004 before making The Show for keeps in 2005. Platooned for part of that year, the second-base job became his when Placido Polanco was traded to the Detroit Tigers. All Utley did was break out with a .291 campaign with 28 home runs and 105 RBIs.

He followed with even better seasons in 2006 (.309 average, 32 home runs, 102 RBIs), 2007 (.332 average, 102 RBIs), 2008 (.292 average, 33 home runs, 104 RBIs), and 2009 (.282 average, 31 home runs, 93 RBIs). He has been voted to five consecutive All Star teams and was the second baseman on *Sports Illustrated*'s MLB All-Decade Team. In 2009, Utley was named No. 6 on the *Sporting News* list of the 50 greatest players in the game.

But Utley is also a hard-nosed player who leads by example. His hustle has made him a fan favorite, and he's repeatedly battled back from injury. Following the 2008 season, he underwent hip surgery that worried some about his ability to be the same player, but he proved the skeptics wrong. Then a diving slide into second base cost him significant time in 2010, limiting him to just 115 games and reducing his offensive effectiveness.

But a healthy Chase Utley in 2011 could very well rekindle those talks about a possible MVP award. He's that good.

The answer to the trivia question about Utley and Oscar Gamble? In the final game at Connie Mack Stadium on October 1, 1970, Gamble was the last player to bat at that hollowed field, driving in Tim McCarver with a game-winning, 10th-inning hit. Then on September 28, 2003, Chase Utley was the last person to bat at Veterans Stadium. The outcome was not as successful as he hit into a game-ending, stadium-closing double play. ∎

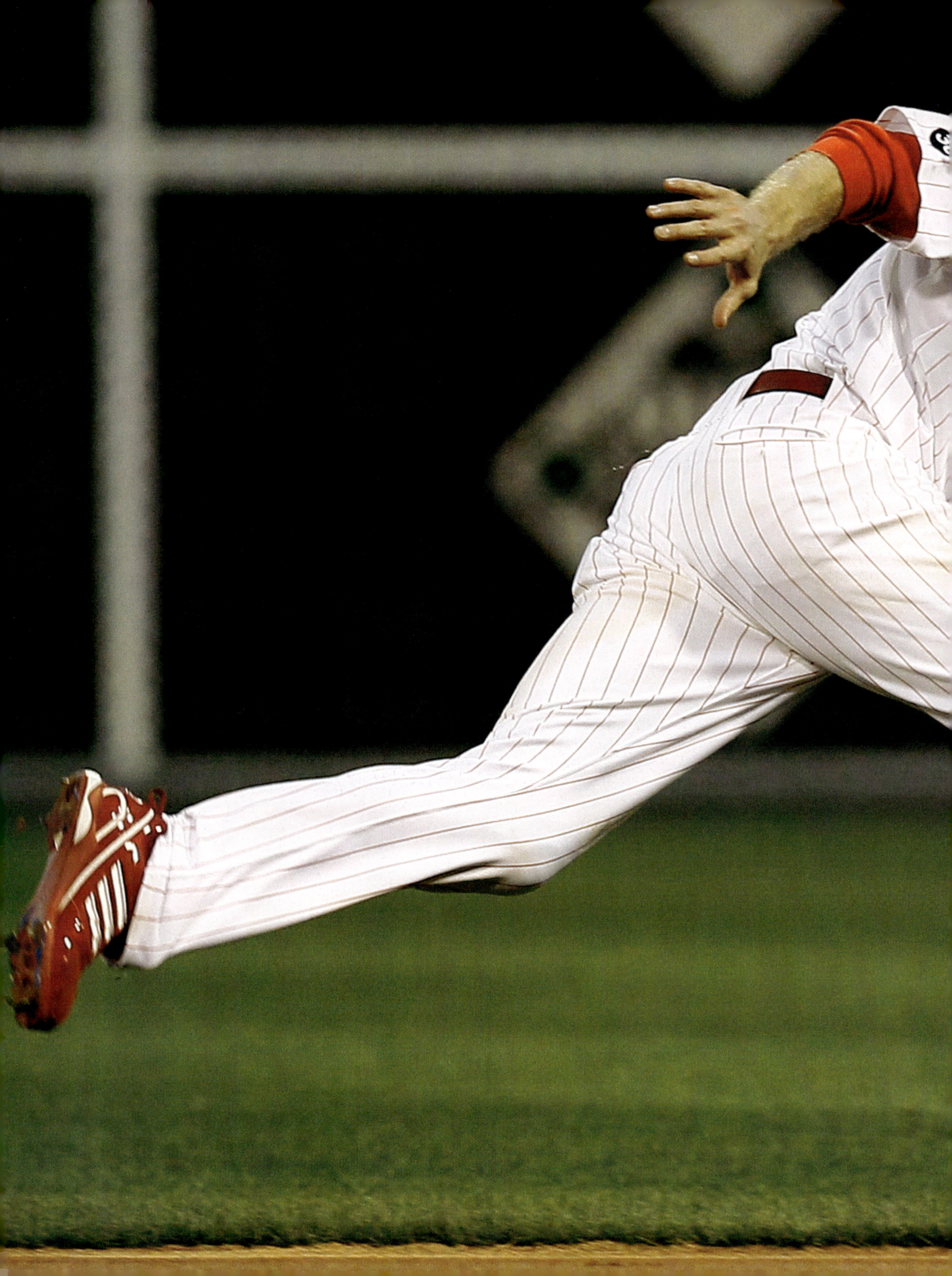

After an abbreviated 2010, the Phillies look forward to having a healthy Chase Utley for the entire 2011 campaign.

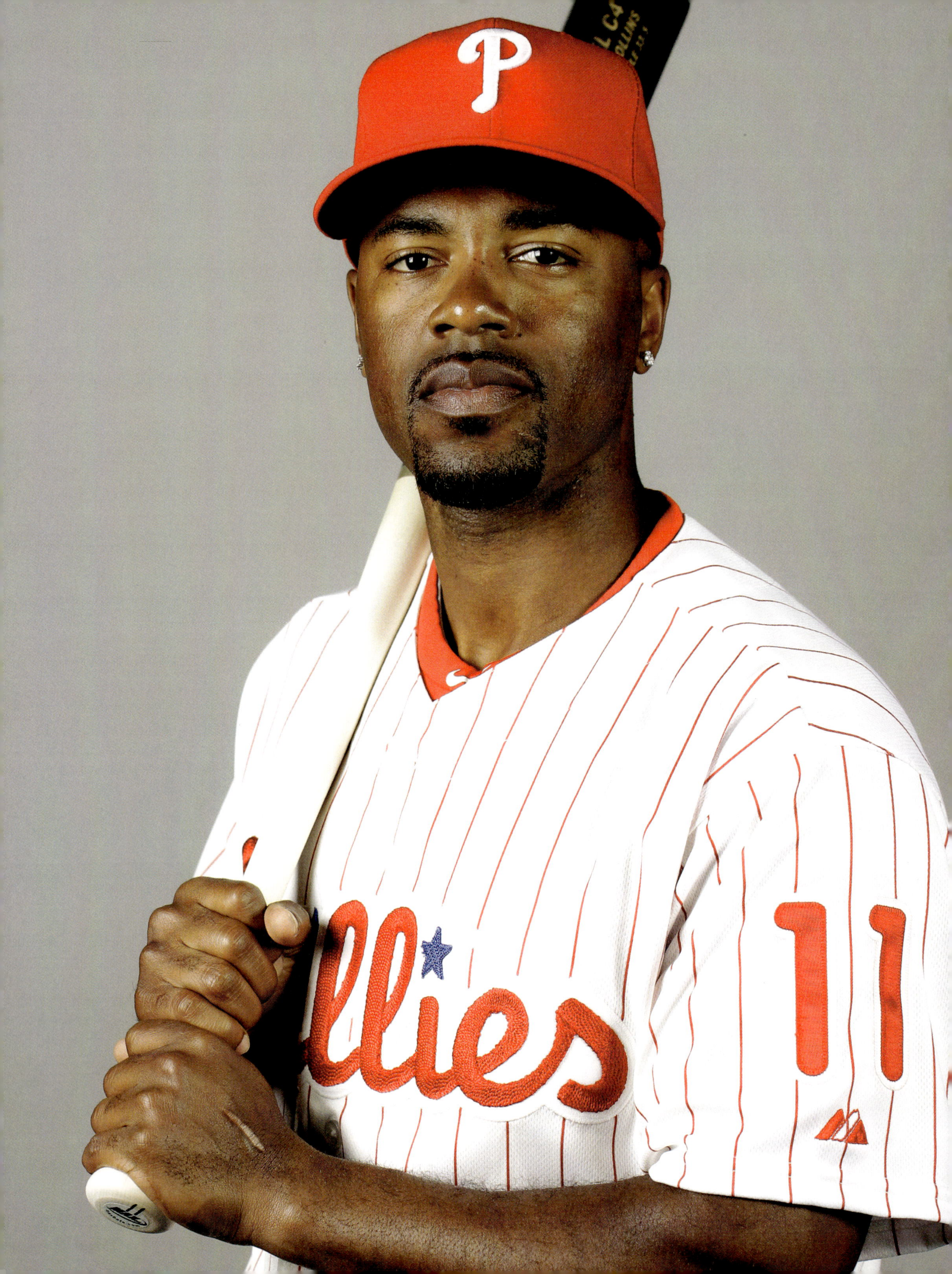
llies
11

Jimmy Rollins — Shortstop

11

	Born: November 27, 1978	Ht: 5'8"	Wt: 170 lbs	B: B	T: R	
	Games	Ave.	Hits	HR	RBI	SB
2010	88	.243	85	8	41	17
Career:	1494	.272	1714	154	662	343

The core of the Phillies' squad is certainly filled with some major performers who lead by example. There is Chase Utley, Ryan Howard, Shane Victorino, Carlos Ruiz, and others. While you could literally list the entire Phillies starting eight as this type of player, Jimmy Rollins leads by example and also is the vocal leader of the Phillies.

On two separate occasions he called out the New York Mets, letting that team and their fans know, as well as the rest of baseball, that the Phillies were the team to beat. To put it bluntly, when you can back it up, it ain't bragging. And Rollins and his teammates have certainly backed it up.

Along with the aforementioned Howard and Utley, Rollins is also a home-grown product of the Phillies' system drafted in the second round of the 1996 draft. You can't teach speed, as they say, and Rollins used his plus speed and outstanding ability to breeze through the minor leagues. Promoted to the Phillies for good in 2001, Rollins responded with a solid .274 season with a league-leading 46 stolen bases. He finished third in Rookie of the Year voting and was a National League All-Star.

A defensive stalwart, Rollins' offensive production started off strong and literally got better each year, culminating in 2007 when he won the National League Most Valuable Player award. He hit .296 with 30 home runs, 38 doubles, 20 triples, 94 RBIs, and 41 stolen bases. He was clearly the best shortstop that the Phillies' franchise had ever had, both offensively and defensively. J-Roll was also a fun and likeable member of the community.

But 2009 was a difficult year as Rollins got off to the worst start at the plate of his career. Mired in a first-half slump, he was hitting just .195 at the end of June. His second half was much better, rallying to finish at .250 with 21 home runs, 77 RBIs, and 31 steals.

Last year, hoping for a big comeback, J-Roll had what might have been the most frustrating season of his career as calf, foot, and hamstring issues limited him to just 88 games and a .243 average. These two subpar years coupled with the fact that Rollins is in the final year of a six-year contract have raised questions about his long-term future in Philadelphia.

Armed & Dangerous

To his credit, he embarked on a new and upgraded off-season workout program to help him stay more limber and injury free. But as players move into their thirties they sometimes see their game begin to diminish.

However, anyone who has seen Jimmy Rollins play over the last decade will find it difficult to believe that his game in diminishing. He is a little older now and needs to train his body differently. Motivation has never been an issue with Rollins and his contract situation will only add fuel to his fire.

Knowing the Jimmy Rollins that fans have enjoyed watching lead the Phillies' team for a decade, there is great hope that he'll be completely healthy in 2011, which should result in a dramatic improvement in his offense. That, in turn, could result in one more contract that will make him a Phillie for the rest of his career. ■

(left) A speedy Jimmy Rollins slides home safely. The 2007 National League MVP was limited to just 88 games in 2010. (above) The popular Rollins signs autographs for fans.

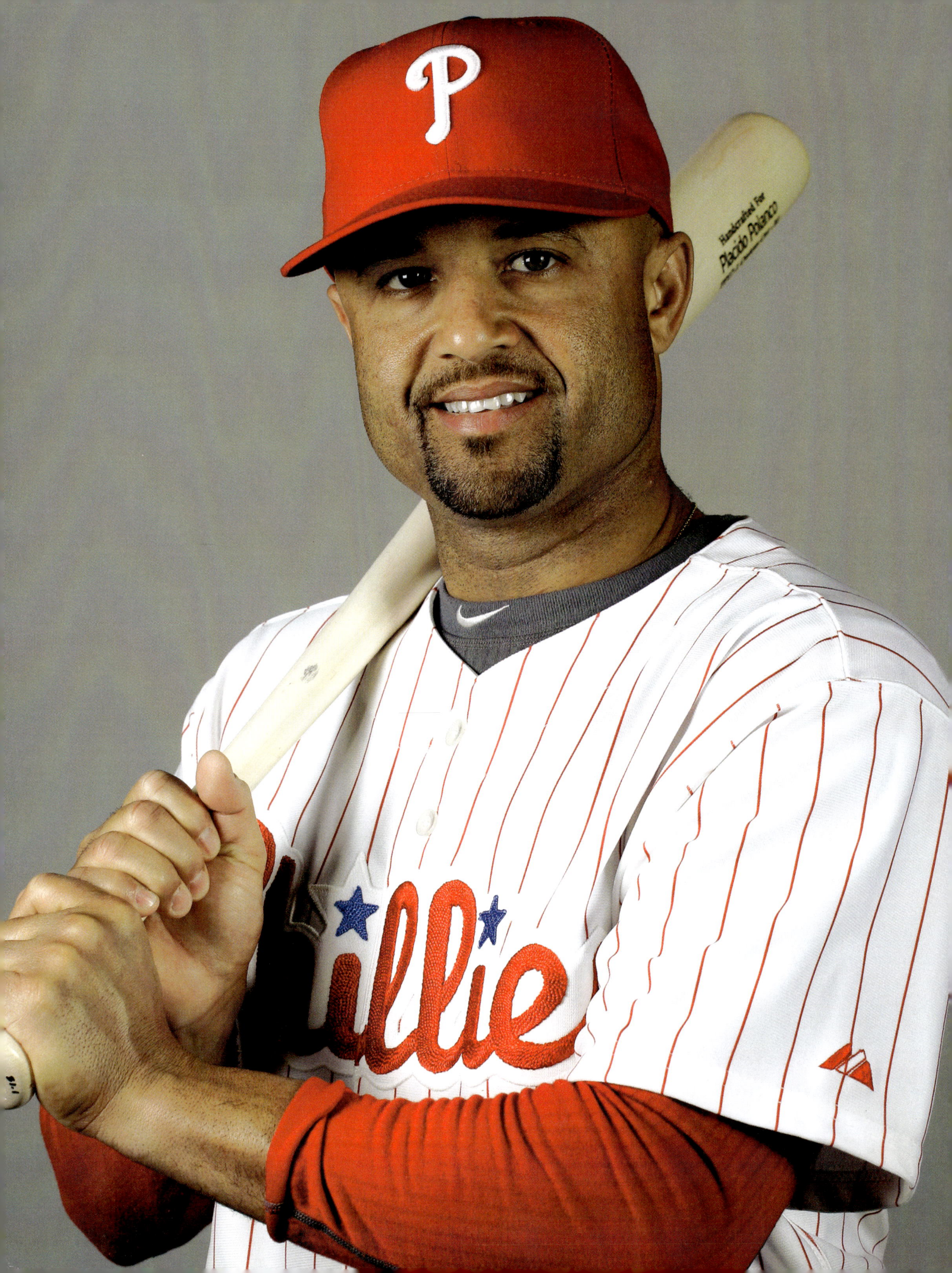
Placido Polanco

27

Placido Polanco — Third Base

Born: October 10, 1975 | Ht: 5'10" | Wt: 190 lbs | B: R | T: R

	Games	Ave.	Hits	HR	RBI	SB
2010:	132	.298	165	6	52	5
Career:	1597	.303	1836	96	631	76

While he's certainly no spring chicken at the age of 36, Placido Polanco is definitely a proven commodity in the world of baseball. Polly, as he's known, is a great contact hitter who will hit for average and be dependable in the clutch. He knows how to play this game. A true professional, he also has the ability to play several infield positions well.

The Phillies needed to replace slick-fielding Pedro Feliz with a little more offensive pop at third base after the 2009 season. Although he was strong defensively with a cannon arm that was very accurate, Feliz did not supply the offensive numbers that the team had hoped for.

So after parting ways with Feliz, allowing him to become a free agent, the club turned to an old friend in Polanco, who had done an outstanding job primarily as a second baseman for the Phillies from 2003 until 2005. He was signed to a three-year contract and gives the team the stability at the hot corner that had been missing.

Polanco did an outstanding job as the Phillies' second baseman, but a budding superstar in Chase Utley needed regular playing time. So the Phillies dispatched Polanco to the Detroit Tigers in exchange for Ugueth Urbina and Ramon Martinez in June 2005. He became a very productive regular at second base in Detroit.

With Feliz gone, the Phillies' brass knew that Polanco had the athletic ability to play third base well and continue his fine offensive performance. He has hit better than .300 five times during his 13-year major league career and barely missed three times, hitting .298 twice and .295 once. He is steady, dependable, and like so many other players on the team, comes to work with his lunch pail every day.

Polanco also is a very stable player at third base who has more than adequately replaced Feliz, filling in and upgrading an already All-Star quality infield. ∎

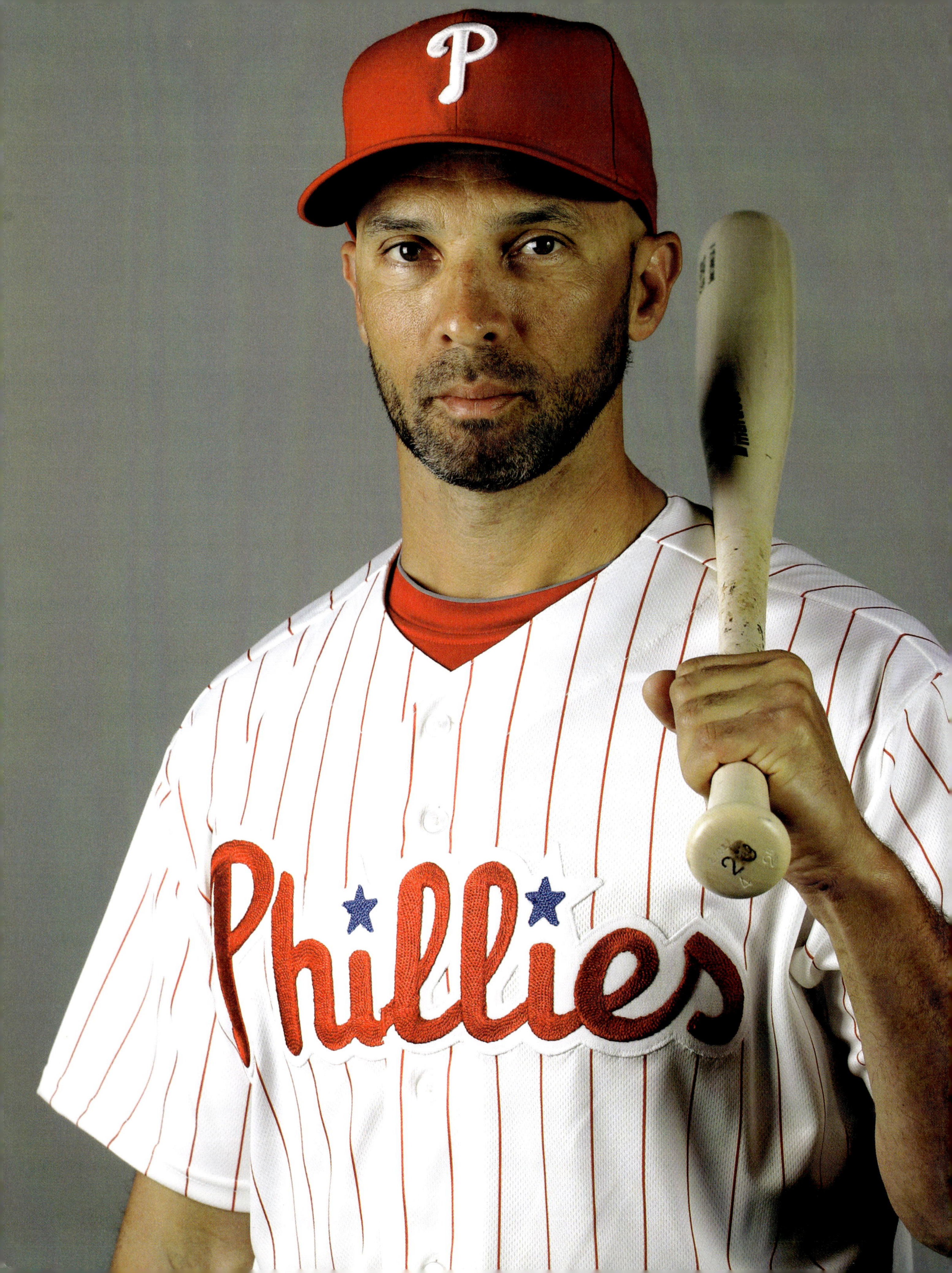
Phillies

Raul Ibanez — Left Field

Born: June 2, 1972 | Ht: 6'2" | Wt: 225 lbs | B: L | T: R

	Games	Ave.	Hits	HR	RBI	SB
2010:	155	.275	154	16	83	4
Career:	1673	.284	1660	232	970	42

Elvis has left the building! That is, the English Bulldog Elvis who just happens to be the pet of former Phillies left fielder Pat Burrell. A mainstay on the club for nine seasons, the popular Burrell was not brought back to the team following the 2008 World Championship win. Signed to replace him on December 16, 2008 was Raul Ibanez.

A veteran left-handed hitter with plenty of pop in his bat, Ibanez had enjoyed a successful career in the American League with Kansas City and Seattle. In 13 seasons in the American League, he hit at a .286 clip with 182 home runs and 794 RBIs. From 2006 through 2008, he averaged 26 homers and 113 RBIs for the Mariners. But when Seattle chose not to re-sign him, the Phillies were there in a heartbeat.

Overall Ibanez has had six seasons with 20 or more home runs and 90 or more RBIs. He also enjoyed a streak of nine consecutive seasons with 30 or more doubles. Ibanez is a hitter with power to the alleys who hits for a high average. Not a bad combination.

In 2009 Ibanez responded to his new surroundings by hitting .272 with 34 home runs (a career high), and 93 RBIs. But in addition he quieted a pair of questions. First, he hit left-handed pitching well, which made for continuity in the batting order. Then he went out and played a very strong and secure left field. Once again, here was another deal that made general manager Ruben Amaro Jr. look like a genius.

While his power numbers were significantly down in 2010, going from 34 homers to just 16, he maintained a solid batting average and was a clutch performer, driving in 83 runs. As he enters the final year of his three-year contract, there is no doubt that Ibanez would like to put together a big season to earn another deal, be it in Philadelphia or elsewhere. ■

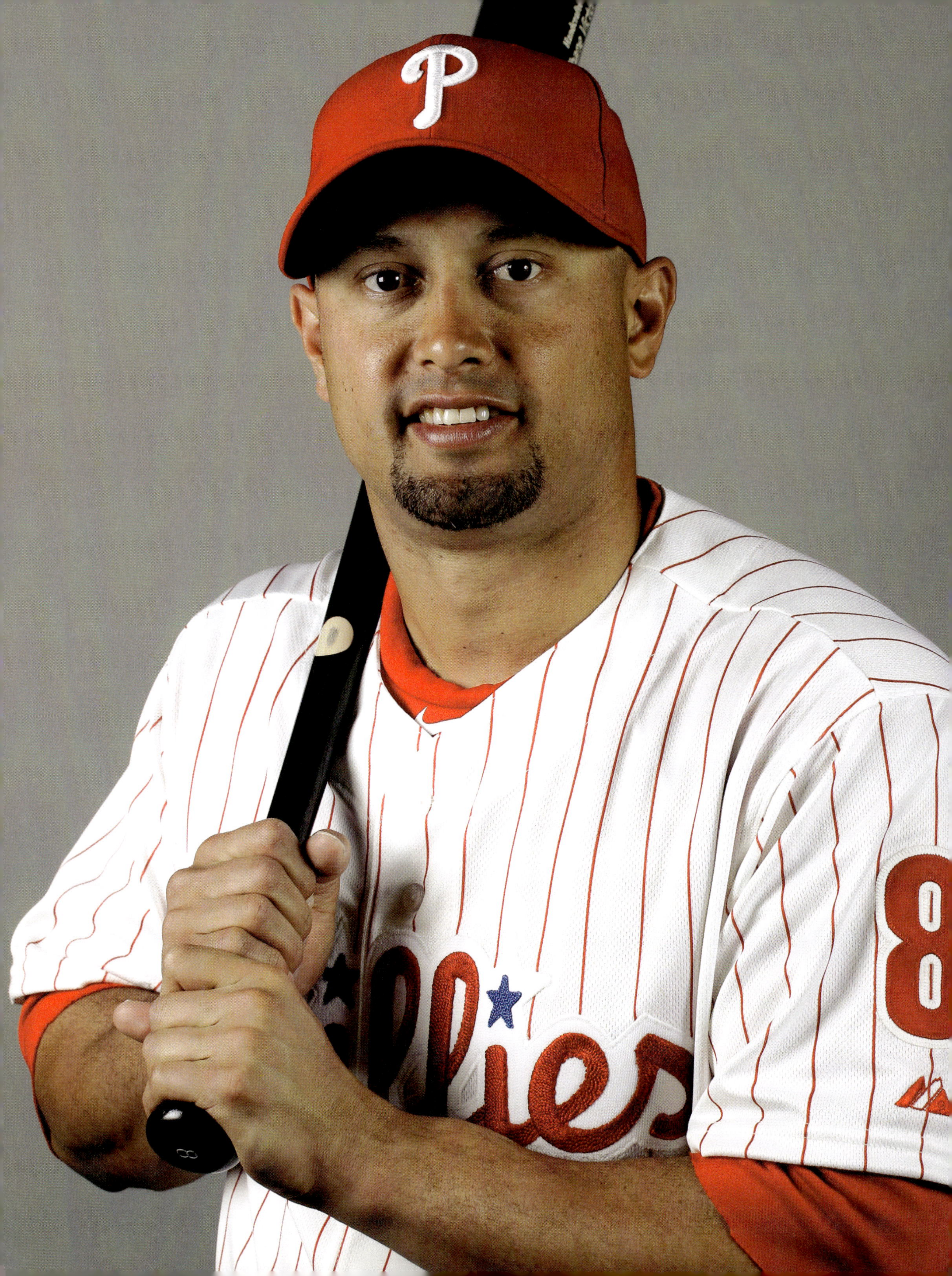

8
Shane Victorino — Center Field

Born: November 30, 1980 | Ht: 5'9" | Wt: 190 lbs | B: B | T: R

	Games	Ave.	Hits	HR	RBI	SB
2010:	147	.259	152	18	69	34
Career:	790	.279	763	62	293	143

The Flyin' Hawaiian has certainly become a household name in Philadelphia. The switch-hitting outfielder always had the tools, he just needed the chance to prove his worth, and that's exactly what happened in Philadelphia.

The talented—but raw—player was chosen by the San Diego Padres from the Los Angeles Dodgers as a Rule 5 pick prior to the 2003 season. Much like pitcher David Herndon from last year's squad, Rule 5 players must stay on the major league roster for the entire season or be offered back to their old team. Struggling with the Padres, hitting just .151 after 36 games, he was offered back to the Dodgers, who accepted him back into their system.

Unable to crack the Dodgers' roster, Victorino split time between Double A and Triple A, and was once again available in 2005 and the Phillies made him a Rule 5 draft choice. He played well in the spring but was unable to crack the starting lineup. He was once again offered back to the Dodgers, who refused. So Victorino was optioned to Triple A Scranton/Wilkes-Barre where he hit .310 with 18 home runs, 70 RBIs, and 17 steals.

A regular with the Phillies in 2006, he smacked the ball at a .287 clip with six homers, 46 RBIs, and added four steals. Not only that but Victorino continually exhibited a fantastic arm from the outfield, repeatedly cutting down opposing base runners attempting to advance on him. He has 24 outfield assists during his career.

Victorino continued to improve in 2007 as he became a more well-rounded big-league player. Blessed with great speed, new first base and base running coach Davey Lopes took the Flyin' Hawaiian under his wings. The result was 37 stolen bases to go along with his .281 batting average, 12 home runs, and 46 RBIs.

In the Phillies' championship season of 2008, Victorino was once again a key performer, hitting a career-high .293 with 14 home runs, 58 RBIs, and 36 stolen bases. The 2009 season saw similar numbers as well as a continuation of his excellence in center field.

When discussing the names of players who had

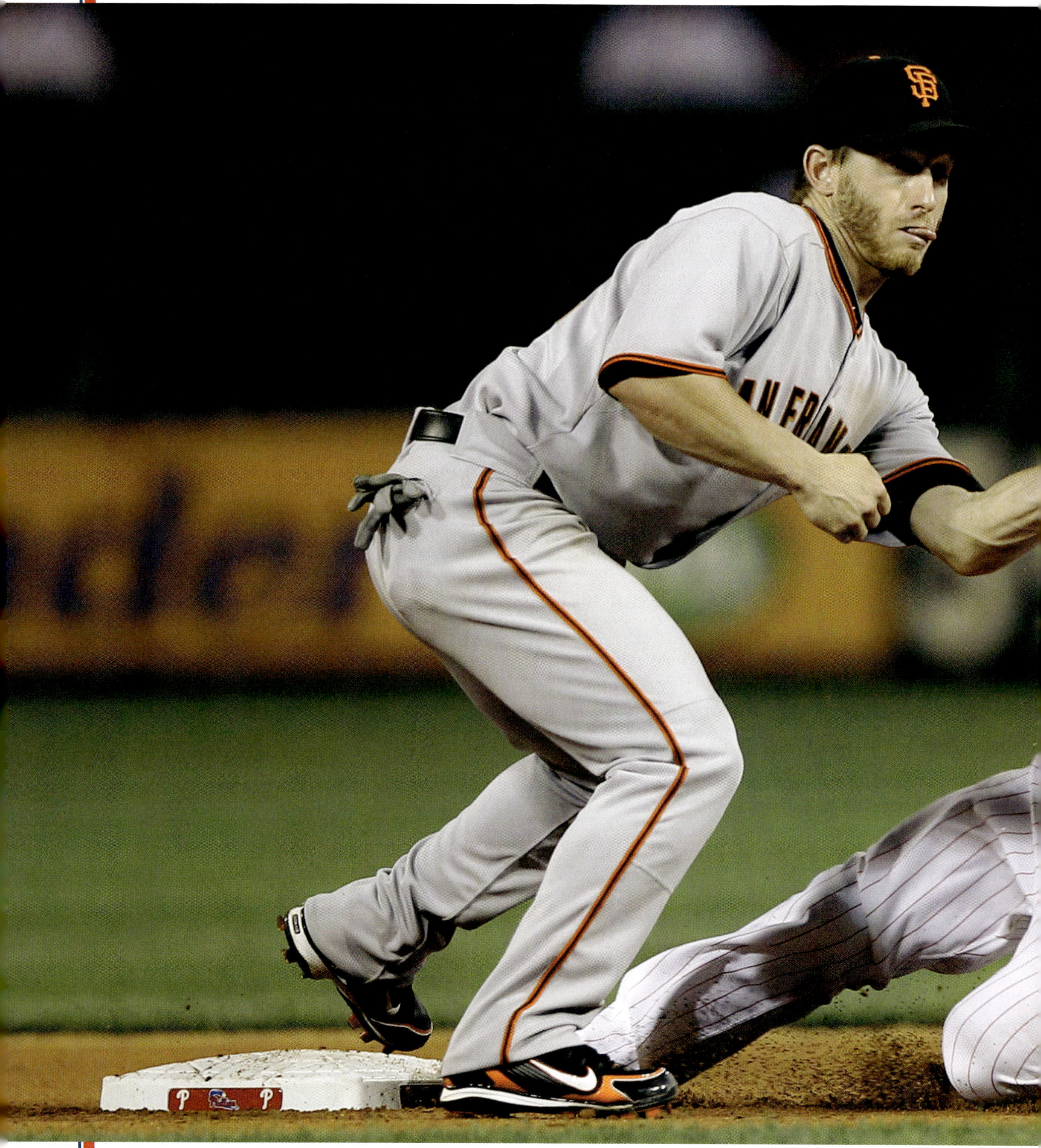

The 2011 Phillies: Perfectly Pitched & Poised to Dominate

disappointing years in 2010, Victorino's name has to appear on the list. While he hit a career-high 18 home runs with 69 RBIs and 34 steals, he batted just .259. The manager hinted that a degree of complacency may have entered into his game as it seemed as though he had trouble focusing at various times during the season. This was an observation that Victorino scoffed at, stating that he felt his mental approach to the game was as consistent as ever.

The fact is that he has been a solid performer ever since his arrival in Philadelphia. If Shane Victorino can rebound and put it together again in 2011, it will go a long way toward helping his team win its fifth straight National League East crown and possibly returning to the Fall Classic. ■

(left) Shane Victorino beats the throw to second base. The speedy center fielder has topped 30 stolen bases in three of his five full big-league seasons. (above) Victorino playfully attacks teammate Ryan Howard with a shaving cream towel after Howard hit a game-winning home run to beat the Reds in July 2010.

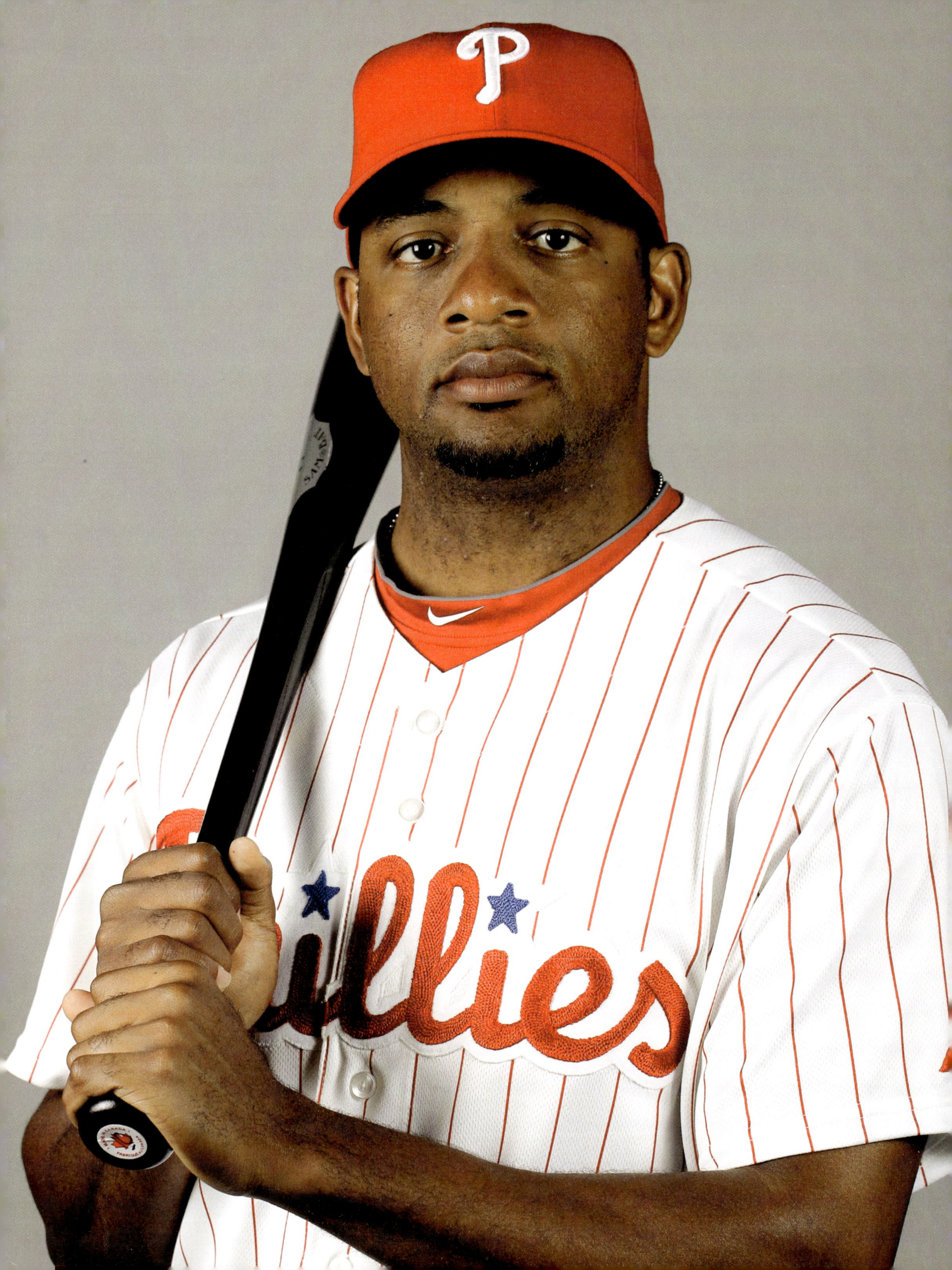

10
Ben Francisco — Right Field

Born: October 23, 1981 | Ht: 6'1" | Wt: 190 lbs | B: R | T: R

	Games	Ave.	Hits	HR	RBI	SB
2010:	88	.268	48	6	28	8
Career:	360	.263	288	39	140	26

Ben Francisco seems like one of those players who has tons of potential but can't get much of an opportunity to display it. Acquired by the Phillies from the Cleveland Indians in July 2009 in the deal that brought Cliff Lee to the Phillies (the first time), Francisco hit .278 in 37 games with five homers and 13 RBIs. Throughout his minor league career, particularly at the Triple A level, he has shown the ability to hit for good average and power. Up to this point he has had limited opportunities to show his wares on the big-league level, with one exception.

In 2008 Francisco got into 121 games for the Indians. He hit .266 with 15 homers and 54 RBIs. In limited playing time the following year he hit another 10 homers. So the ability seems to be there. All that has been missing has been the opportunity to play on a regular basis.

It appears that the chance to play regularly is there for the taking in 2011. With the departure of Jayson Werth to the Washington Nationals and big bucks, there is a glowing hole in the Phillies' lineup that could really use a right-handed hitter with some power to protect Ryan Howard in the No. 4 spot in the batting order.

Francisco will be fighting challenges from Domonic Brown and John Mayberry Jr. for the bulk of playing time in right field. But if he gets off to a good start and takes advantage of his opportunity, Ben Francisco could well be the regular right fielder in 2011 and beyond.

It was only a few years ago that the Phillies gave a chance to a similarly untested, young outfielder. His name was Jayson Werth. Francisco is hoping that, as far as right field with the Phillies is concerned, history will repeat itself. ∎

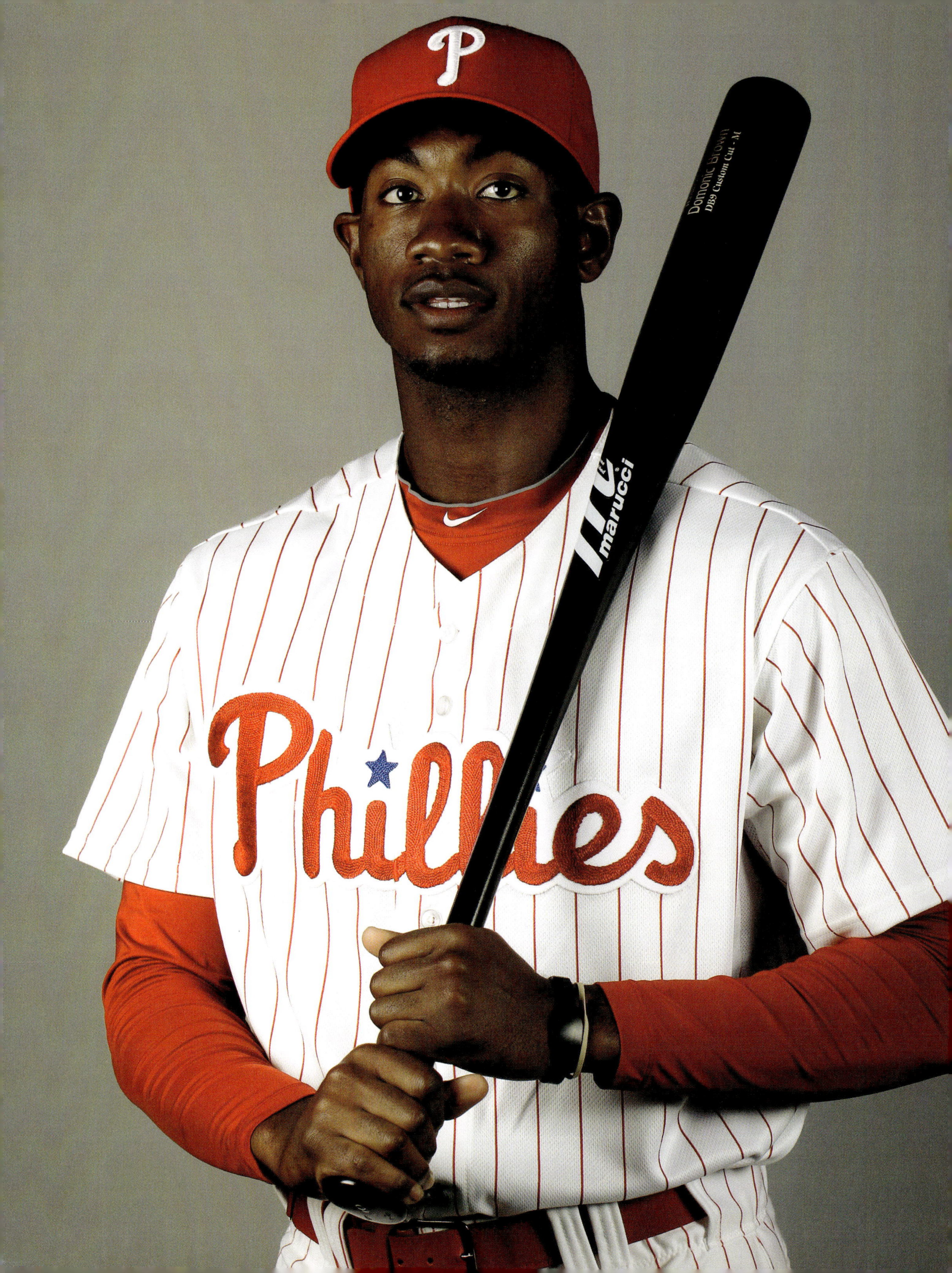
Domonic Brown
DB9 Custom Cut - M
marucci
Phillies

9
Domonic Brown — Right Field

Born: September 3, 1987 | Ht: 6'5" | Wt: 200 lbs | B: L | T: L

	Games	Ave.	Hits	HR	RBI	SB
2010:	35	.210	13	2	13	2

When baseball scouts talk about Domonic Brown they talk in terms of a five-tool player who can run, hit for average, hit for power, field well, and throw well. This lanky outfield prospect certainly seems like a future big-league star.

The 20th round draft choice in the 2006 amateur draft worked his way through the Phillies' minor league system. Earning an invitation to spring training in 2010, Brown played well. Opening the season at Double A Reading, he hit .318 in 65 games with 15 home runs, 47 RBIs, and 12 stolen bases. Promoted to Triple A Lehigh Valley, he continued his fine play, hitting .346 in 28 games with five homers, 21 RBIs, and five stolen bases.

When Shane Victorino went on the disabled list on July 28, Brown was called up to the big club to fill in. Getting an RBI double in his first major league at bat, he showed flashes of real talent. But he rarely played down the stretch, causing some to think that Brown might have been better served by returning to Triple A where he could play every day.

With Francisco seemingly ready to step into Werth's shoes in right field, there is no immediate need for Brown to be put into a platoon situation on the major league level. While that may happen, he might be better served by being a regular at Lehigh Valley to continue the learning process and build his confidence.

One of the major decisions made by the Phillies this spring will center around right field and who will ultimately win the job. One thing seems certain. Whether or not Domonic Brown makes the team out of spring training or not, he seems to be considered a fixture in the Phillies' outfield of the future. The only question is if the future is now. ∎

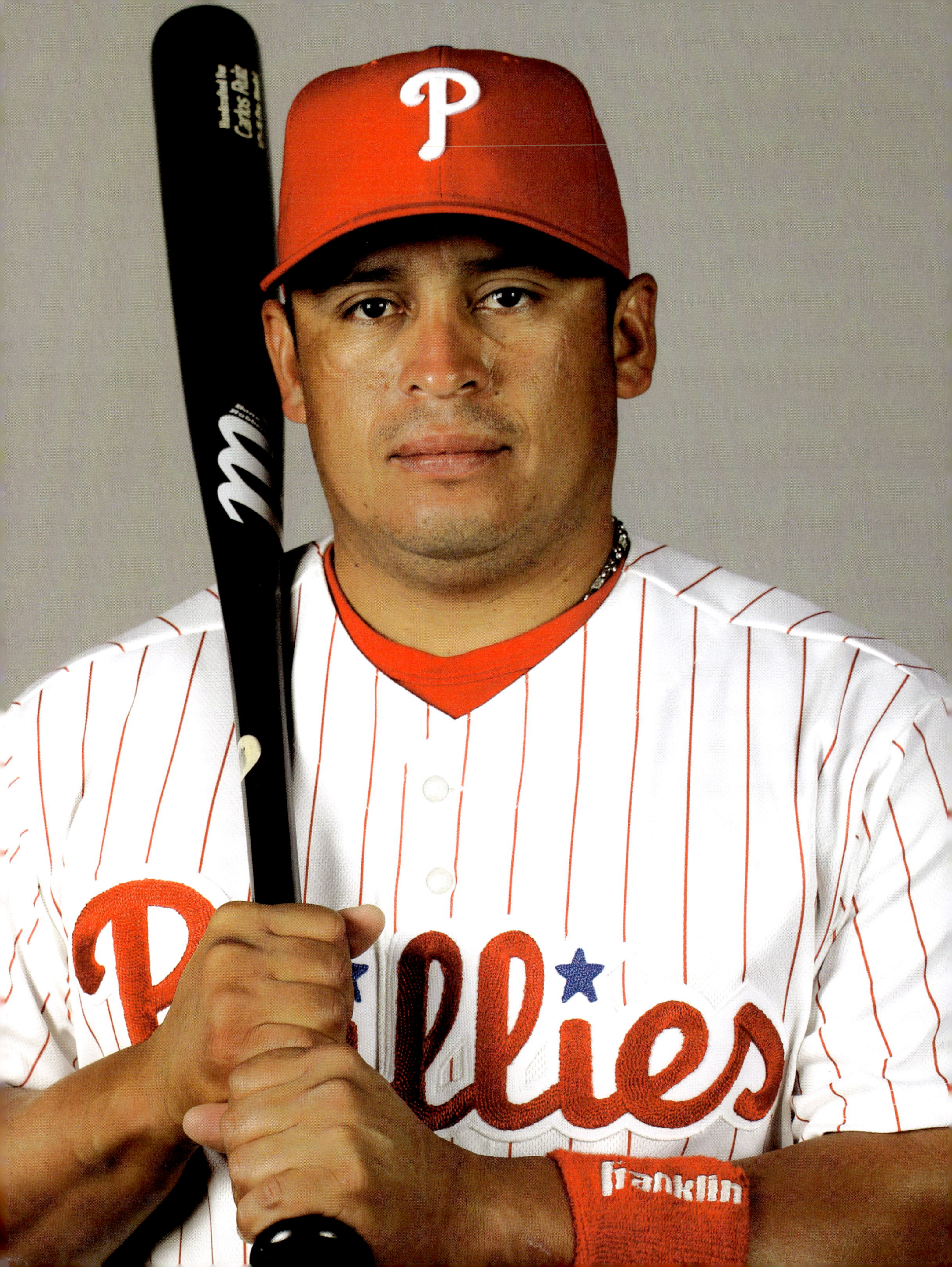
franklin

51
Carlos Ruiz — Catcher

Born: January 22, 1979 | Ht: 5'10" | Wt: 215 lbs | B: R | T: R

	Games	Ave.	Hits	HR	RBI	SB
2010:	121	.302	112	8	53	0
Career:	487	.260	379	30	191	10

Phillies fans have had the opportunity to see Carlos Ruiz grow into a stellar big-league catcher right in front of their eyes. Signed as an amateur free agent by the club in 1998, the stocky backstop climbed up the organizational ladder and first made a name for himself with a solid year in Double A Reading in 2004 in which he hit .294. The following season he hit Triple A pitching at a .300 clip while playing for Scranton/Wilkes-Barre. Chooch, as he is affectionately named, was called up to the big club during the 2006 season before making it for good the following year.

With veteran Rod Barajas and Chris Coste both expecting some playing time behind the plate, 2007 was a breakout year for Ruiz, who hit .259 with six homers and 54 RBIs in 115 games. Although he slumped offensively in 2008, his defense and handling of pitchers improved and he saved his best offensive outbursts for the postseason, hitting over .300 in both the National League Championship Series as well as the World Series.

"Ah, he is going to continue getting better," his former battery mate Jamie Moyer said of Chooch with a smile. "I saw this kid come up in '06 and try to get his feet wet. He was very shy, very quiet, and not very sure of himself. You see that happen a lot with young guys coming up. But he took a lot in, was very observant, asked questions, and worked very hard. He really cares about his catching and he cares about his pitchers. I think that is quite evident in how he handles the staff and he has turned into a great catcher. He's Latin and I think that there might have been a communications barrier with him at first. That's not an issue anymore."

Ruiz has blossomed into one of the most respected backstops in the game. While he'll probably never put Johnny Bench offensive numbers up there, he is

Armed & Dangerous

The 2011 Phillies: Perfectly Pitched & Poised to Dominate

known for his ability to get clutch hit after clutch hit and for playing the game the right way.

"His hitting is so clutch. And that is something that separates him from a lot of catchers. Just think of all the key hits he has contributed over the last couple of years. That is what's so special about the whole team. Everybody on the team contributes. Not just three or four guys. With the Phillies, you have 25 guys who can really influence the team."

On the heels of his first .300 season at the plate in 2010 and as a catcher entering his prime, Jamie Moyer could very well be correct. Chooch could get better and better over the next couple of seasons. ■

Carlos Ruiz is respected as an outstanding defensive catcher and known his skills in calling a game. In 2010 he turned heads by posting a .302 batting average.

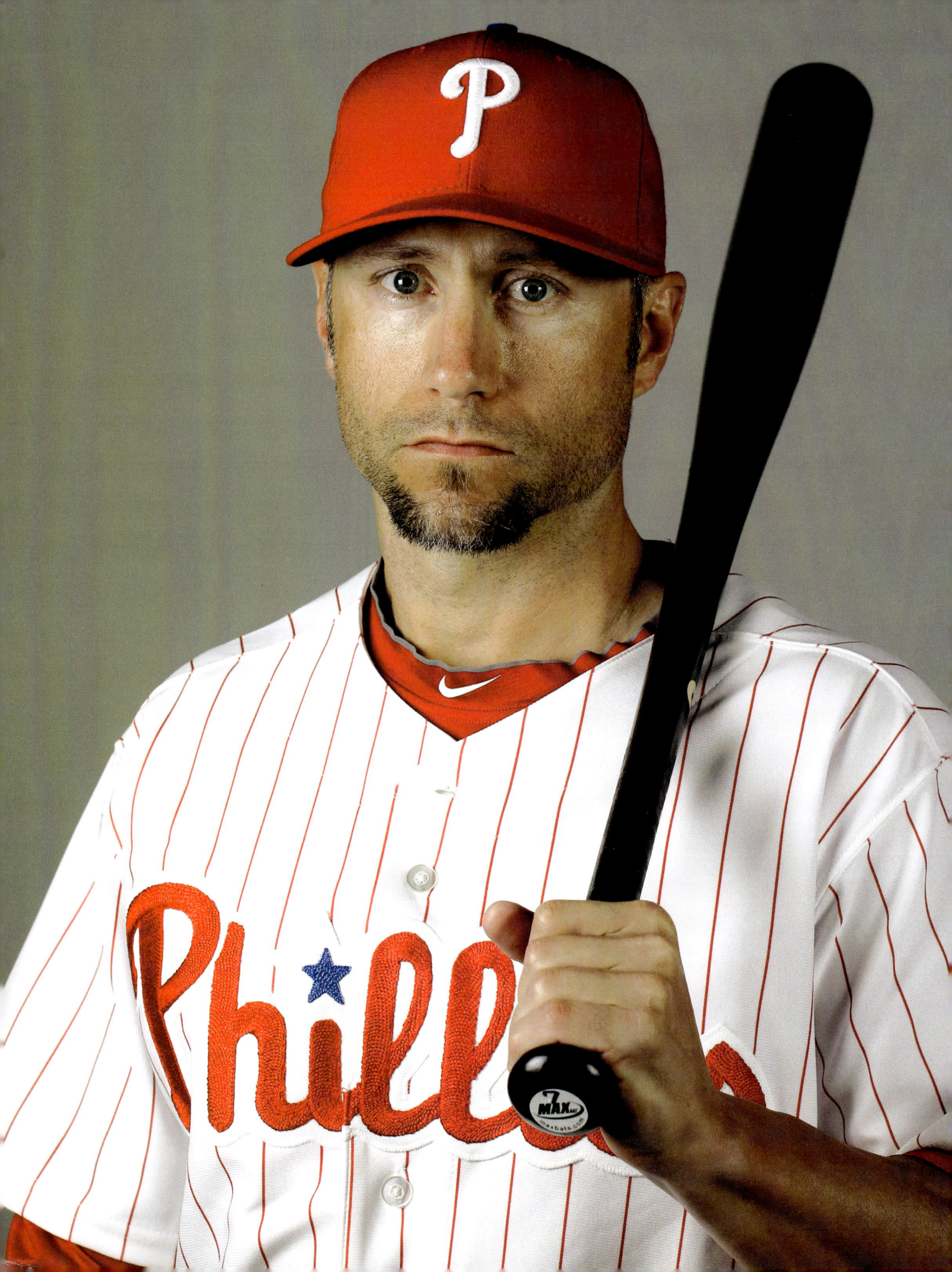

21 Wilson Valdez | 7 Ross Gload
23 Brian Schneider | 40 John Mayberry Jr.

There are two schools of thought about players coming off the bench to augment a solid lineup. These players could be talented enough to start on most teams and will chomp at the bit to get some game action. Of course, that desire to play more can cause a problem occasionally. And then there are players who can play well, but might have problems with certain kinds of pitching, or are just better coming off the bench. It seems like the Phillies' bench this year will have a little bit of both. Their super-subs are all talented enough to crack the starting nine of some teams. But on a deep, World Series—contending team such as Philadelphia, they will be role players who will need to be ready in case of injury.

Last year, injuries happened. The biggest concern came with a succession of injuries to Jimmy Rollins, who was limited to just 88 games. Thankfully for the Phillies, Wilson Valdez won himself a job on the team and filled in very adequately for J-Roll. He hit .258 in 111 games with four home runs and 35 RBIs. He was also very solid at shortstop and has an absolute howitzer for an arm.

Just to put his season into a career perspective, after beating out Juan Castro for the utility role during the season, Valdez had career highs in games, at-bats, runs, hits, total bases, doubles, triples, RBIs, walks, intentional walks, stolen bases, strikeouts, and slugging percentage.

Obviously, if he does not match those numbers in 2011 then Phillies will probably be better off, because that means their regulars won't be missing as much time. But after stops with the Chicago White Sox, Seattle Mariners, San Diego Padres, Los Angeles Dodgers, and the New York Mets, for as much as it's possible for a utility player to do so, it could be that Wilson Valdez has found a home.

Ross Gload.

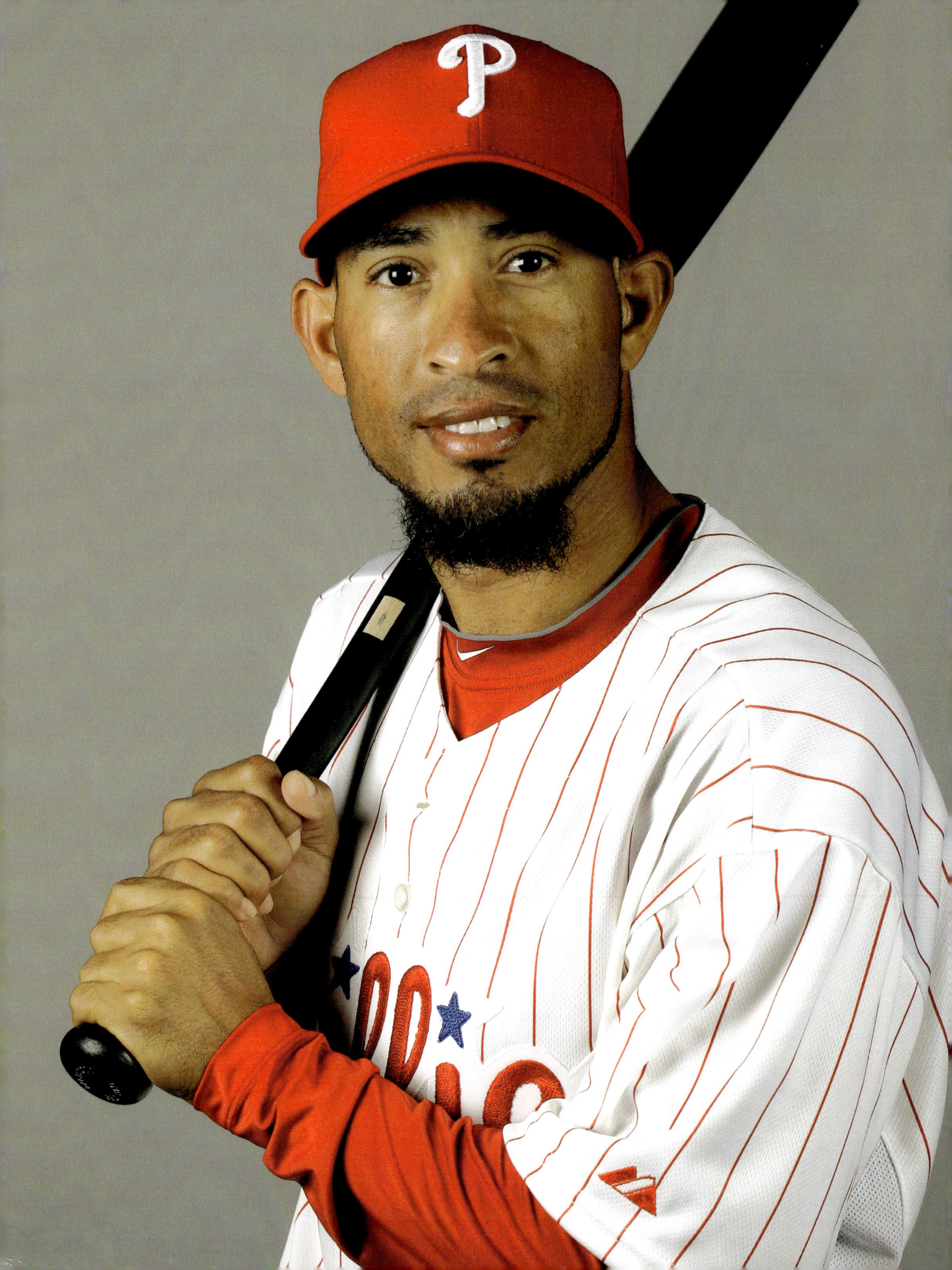

For a number of years, the Phillies were lucky enough to have a great left-handed bat off the bench in Gregg Dobbs. From 2007 to 2009, he was as good as you can get in that role. But after some slippage in Dobbs' production, the Phils signed veteran Ross Gload as a free agent. Gload came into town and excelled in the role as his .281 average in 94 games would indicate. He also contributed six home runs and 22 RBIs. With Dobbs moving on to the Florida Marlins, Ross Gload is secure in his spot on the Phillies' bench.

Catcher Brian Schneider had been a thorn in the side of the Phillies for years. During his 10-year big-league run with the Montreal Expos, Washington Nationals, and New York Mets, this .251 career hitter seemed to save his best games for when he was playing against the Phillies. Going to high school in the Philadelphia suburbs made each game against the Phillies a home game of sorts. Now, every Phillies game for Schneider is a home game.

Subbing for Carlos Ruiz, there was not much opportunity for Schneider to make a huge impact in 2010. In just 47 games he hit .240 with four home runs and 15 RBIs. But he has been a steady performer behind the plate during his big-league career and gives the Phillies and Charlie Manuel every confidence that if Ruiz needs a break, or should he be injured, that Brian Schneider is a more-than-capable backup.

John Mayberry Jr. looks like a baseball player. At 6'6", 235 pounds, with a great arm and power at the plate, the son of the former big league first baseman, John Mayberry, Jr. seems to have all the qualities needed to become a regular fixture on a major league team.

The first round draft pick of the Texas Rangers in 2005, Mayberry was dealt to the Phillies in exchange for highly-touted Greg Golson. In two short stints with the Phillies, Mayberry has hit .232 with six home runs and 14 RBIs. The ability is there. And it seems that there is a roster spot for the taking on the 2011 Phillies.

It will be interesting to see if John Mayberry Jr. steps up and takes that spot. So while the Phillies' bench has some players who fit perfectly into the role of a guy who comes off the bench to make a contribution, others like Mayberry still have the opportunity to vie for a regular spot in the lineup.

With the Phillies' bench, it's the perfect blend. ■

Wilson Valdez.

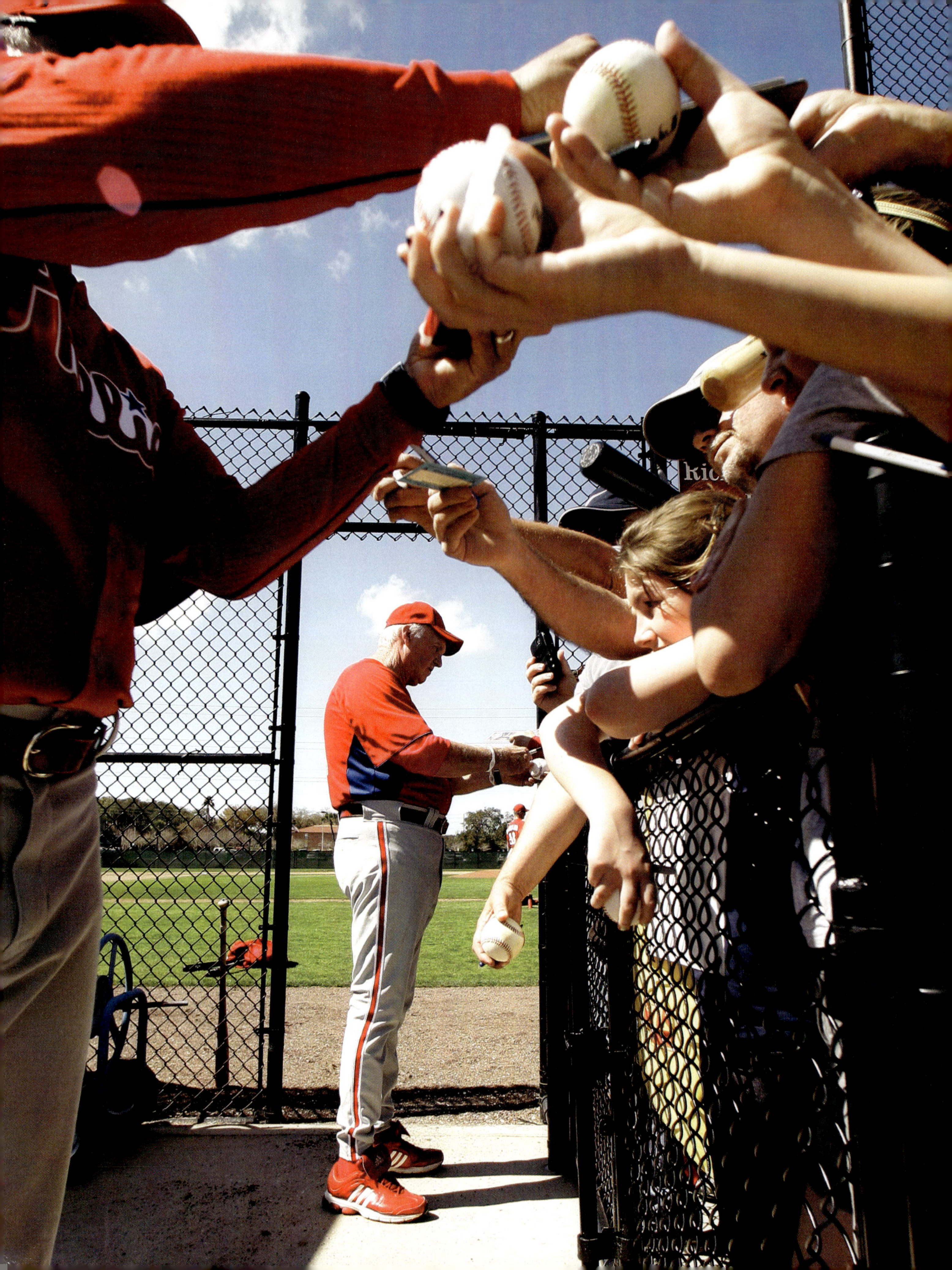

5

Charlie Manuel — The Skipper

The fact is, Charlie Manuel has become an icon among Philadelphia sports fans. And as anyone familiar with that particular group will tell you, it's not an easy thing to do. Hired to replace popular Larry Bowa as Phillies manager prior to the 2005 season, he was on the proverbial short leash. Bowa, a longtime Phillies player and coach prior to his elevation to the helm of the team, epitomized the prototypical Philadelphia fan-favorite athlete. He was a blue-collar player who had more heart than ability and who wore his heart on his sleeve.

In truth, Big Chuck, as he is known on the team, replaced Gary Varsho as manager of the team. Varsho managed the final game of the 2004 season after Bowa's dismissal.

Manuel is a guy who is easy to underestimate. He is a big, ol' country boy from Northfork, West Virginia, who has a relaxed manner and a southern drawl second to none. At first glance, you don't see the intensity of a Bowa. But as Big Chuck has proven, he deserves more than simply a first glance. He has an inner fire and desire to win equal to Bowa or anyone else.

A two-sport star in high school with grades good enough to attend the University of Pennsylvania, Manuel spurned offers from the Pittsburgh Pirates, Detroit Tigers, and New York Yankees to sign a free-agent contract with the Minnesota Twins in 1963.

Working his way through the Twins' minor league system, he earned a spot on the Twins team that reached the playoffs in 1969. He hit .207 with the big club with a pair of home runs and 24 RBIs in 83 games. He was on the bubble between Triple A and the Twins over the next three seasons before playing briefly for the Los Angeles Dodgers in 1974 and 1975.

That was the time when Manuel made what may have been the best decision of his playing career when he signed a contract with the Yakult Swallows

Charlie Manuel signs autographs during spring training practice on February 23, 2011, in Clearwater, Florida.

Armed & Dangerous

The 2011 Phillies: Perfectly Pitched & Poised to Dominate

in Japan. In his six seasons playing in Japan for Yakult and the Kinetsu Buffaloes, he hit .303 with 189 home runs and 491 RBIs. In his two greatest seasons, Aka-oni (the red devil, as he was known), hit .324 in 1979 with a league-leading 37 home runs and 94 RBIs in a season in which he became the first American player to be named the Pacific League MVP. The following season, he smacked the ball at a .325 clip and led the league with 48 home runs and 129 RBIs.

"If I had never gone and played baseball in Japan," Manuel said, "I don't think I would have been a coach or manager. I learned to respect things more. I think that their ways, their discipline, their culture, and things like that was something I took time not only to learn myself, but I learned that there [are] more peo-

(left) A relaxed Phillies manager Charlie Manuel addresses the media during a new conference. (above) Manuel lets umpire Greg Gibson know his opinion of a call Gibson made in an August 2011 game against the Astros.

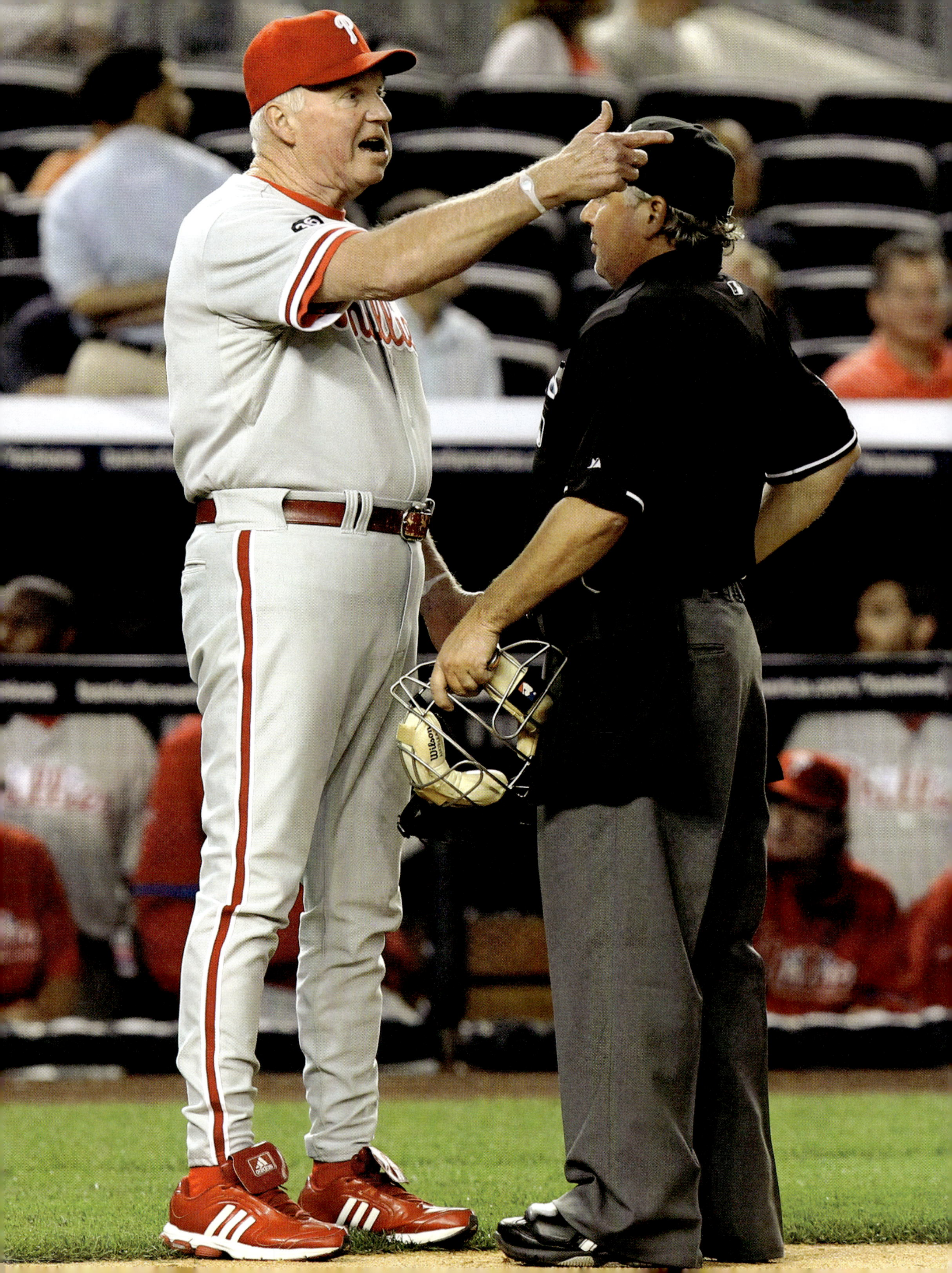

ple in the world than Charlie Manuel. I think that is where I really became in control of myself and everything became positive for me in baseball."

Manuel returned to the United States following his playing career and began a nine-year managing career in the minor leagues that took him to such teams as Wisconsin, Orlando, Toledo, Portland, Colorado Springs, and Charlotte. He then spent two-plus seasons as the skipper of the Cleveland Indians, who reached the World Series under his tenure.

He joined the Phillies as special assistant to the general manager and was named the team's 51st manager. His 2005 squad finished in second place with an 88–74 record, which was the highest victory total for a first-year Phillies manager since Pat Corrales won 89 games in 1982.

The following season, 2006, Manuel's charges won three fewer games and finished once again in second place. While there was continued frustration in the Delaware Valley over the club's inability to get over that second-place hump, it was also noted that Manuel's 173–151 record in his first two seasons as manager of the Phillies was the most wins of any team skipper in franchise history since Pat Moran had 181 wins in 1915–1916. Clearly, something special was going on at Citizens Bank Park.

"The thing I like about Charlie is that he lets guys play and lets you do your thing in the clubhouse," said Jamie Moyer. "He is always within reach. If something is not working, he gives you the opportunity to fix it, but if you can't, he has answer about how to fix it and helps you be better. He stays

(left) Charlie Manuel discusses a ninth-inning call with umpire Tom Hallion during a 2010 interleague game against the Yankees in New York. (above) Manuel talks to San Francisco Giants coach Shawon Dunston before Game 6 of the 2010 National League Championship Series.

Armed & Dangerous

> **"With Charlie, what you see is what you get. To me that is important. I don't like being around people who make you feel like you have to walk on eggshells."**
>
> —Longtime Phillies broadcaster Chris Wheeler

in character. Charlie is a baseball man through and through. He eats, sleeps, and drinks baseball. He's just an old baseball player who became a manager. His door is always open, which is something else I respect about him. You can have a lot of fun with Charlie, but he can be serious, too."

Amidst high hopes in 2007, the team got off to a rough start and played inconsistently. But after Manuel called out a controversial Philadelphia radio host who repeatedly questioned the manager about not challenging his underachieving players while insulting him personally, the team went on a five-game winning streak. And down the stretch, the Phillies went on a 23–11 streak to overtake the floundering New York Mets to capture the National League Eastern Division crown. Even though they were swept in the playoffs by the Colorado Rockies, there was a feeling that better things were just over the horizon.

The 2008 campaign saw a doggedly determined

Charlie Manuel's Phillies have captured four consecutive National League East titles.

Armed & Dangerous

Philadelphia Phillies team that spoke often of unfinished business. Another late-season New York Mets slump, coupled with a strong Phillies finish saw the locals once again overtake New York to win the division with a 92–70 record.

In the National League Division Series the Phillies ousted a talented Milwaukee Brewers team, and then defeated the Los Angeles Dodgers in the NLCS to earn their first World Series berth since 1993. The rest is history, as they say, as the Phillies defeated the Tampa Bay Rays in five games to win the second World Series championship in franchise history. The only other one had come 28 years previously in 1980.

Suddenly, Charlie Manuel was the toast of the town. The love affair between the Phils skipper and the City of Brotherly Love was nowhere near over.

Broadcaster Chris Wheeler has seen many men fill the shoes of the manager of the Philadelphia Phillies during his long tenure with the team, with varying degrees of success and failure. But Charlie Manuel is one of a kind. He was clearly the right man for the right team at the right time.

"With Charlie, what you see is what you get," he said. "To me that is important. I don't like being around people who make you feel like you have to walk on eggshells. I don't like that, and he's not like that at all. To me, he's the same every day. The players see and appreciate that consistency, too. He brings that day in and day out and promotes a positive attitude in the clubhouse. It is such a long season that is so predicated on failing that you need a positive guy there. He has his bad days, but they know who the boss is and where they stand with him."

The standing of the team continued to grow into the 2009 season. Winning a World Series will do that for you. A return engagement to the Fall Classic ended in defeat at the hands of the New York Yankees, but Charlie Manuel became the first manager in Phillies franchise history to lead his team to consecutive World Series appearances.

With the addition of Roy Halladay at the top of the Phillies' rotation, hopes were high for a hat trick in 2010. The mid-season addition of Roy Oswalt only strengthened an already impressive pitching staff. The team won its fourth consecutive National League East title with a 97–65 record, but were upset in the postseason by the upstart San Francisco Giants, the eventual World Series winners.

In his six years as skipper of the Phillies, Manuel has a 544–428 record for a .560 winning percentage. Coupled with his time at the helm of the Cleveland Indians, his career managerial record is 764–618. He is clearly a guy you don't want to underestimate. ■

Charlie Manuel argues with home plate umpire CB Bucknor after during the 10th inning of a June 2010 game in Cincinnati. Manuel was ejected.

Armed & Dangerous

Answering questions at the start of spring training, Jimmy Rollins was nothing if not confident in the 2011 Phillies' chances. "Yeah, we'll win 100 games," the Phillies shortstop said. "I really plan on going after, who is it? I know Seattle won 114 or something recently, and I know the record is probably a little more than that, but we'll go get something hopefully in that range."

Phils Trivia Tester

1.) Roy Halladay won the National League Cy Young Award following his stellar 2010 season. Who was the last Phillies pitcher to win that award?

2.) Wilson Valdez was a valuable member of the team in 2010 filling in admirably for both Jimmy Rollins and Chase Utley when they were injured. Who was the utility man that Valdez beat out during the season to earn the reserve spot on the roster?

3.) Name two members of the 2010 Phillies team who grew up in the Philadelphia suburbs.

4.) Charlie Manuel has won 544 games as the manager of the Phillies. In the history of the franchise, only three managers have won more games. Name them.

5.) On June 23, 1971, Phils ace right-hander Rick Wise pitched a no-hitter against the Cincinnati Reds en route to a 4–0 win. But he also made history as the only pitcher to hit two home runs during his no-hitter. Name the two Cincinnati pitchers who surrendered homers to Wise.

6.) Speaking of Rick Wise, during his career he was involved in trades for two Hall of Fame pitchers. Name them.

7.) Ryan Howard was named National League Rookie of the Year in 2005. Which Phillie won that award before Howard?

8.) Phillies outfielder Shane Victorino is known as the Flyin' Hawaiian. But two other natives of the 50th state have played for the Phillies. Name them.

9.) Most Phillies fans know that Charlie Manuel and Dallas Green are the only managers in the history of the franchise to win World Series titles in Philadelphia. But name the managers who Green and Manuel replaced at the helm of the team.

10.) Name the two Phillies who drove in the winning runs in each of their two World Series championship-deciding games and what do they have in common?

Answers: 1.) Steve Bedrosian in 1987 2.) Juan Castro 3.) Jamie Moyer and Brian Schneider 4.) Gene Mauch (646), Harry Wright (636), and Danny Ozark (594) 5.) Ross Grimsley and Clay Carroll 6.) Steve Carlton and Dennis Eckersley 7.) Scott Rolen in 1997 8.) Sid Fernandez and Dane Sardinha 9.) Green replaced Danny Ozark. Manuel replaced Larry Bowa with one game remaining in the 2004 season. 10.) Mike Schmidt in 1980 and Pedro Feliz in 2008. Both played third base.

Roy Halladay and Phillies fans have plenty to be excited about heading into 2011.